AWAKEN
THE DIVINE FEMININE

AWAKENING
THE DIVINE FEMININE
THE PANCHA PRAKRITI GODDESSES

ADI KṚṢṆA RAMA

Motilal Banarsidass Publications

MOTILAL BANARSIDASS
PUBLICATIONS
4741/23, Ansari Road, Daryaganj, New Delhi - 110002 (India)
Email: mlbd@mlbd.com | sales@mlbd.com
exports@mlbd.com | publications@mlbd.com
Website: www.mlbd.com

Awakening the Divine Feminine
by
Adi Kṛṣṇa Rama

Reprint, 2026
First Edition Published in 2024

Published in India by Motilal Banarsidass Publications

ISBN : 978-81-97087-05-9 (PB)

Printed and bound in India

Contents

Part Two
Questions to the Master

Part Three
Guidance for Practices

Contents

Foreword

Editing this book has been a transformative journey for me. I was immediately intrigued by the depth of the author's understanding of the transformational process. His work carries the clarity and sharp edge of intellect as the works of Krishnamurti, while reading it invokes the same meditative and heart-awakening experience that one feels reading Osho's teachings. Throughout my life, I have delved into countless personal growth and spiritual guidance books, but very few reach the level of profundity and directness found in this work. In today's era of social media jargon and commodification of spirituality, finding such authentic guidance is nearly impossible.

It has been an honour to work on this book. As a medical doctor with extensive experience in psychology and psychiatry, I can attest to the author's ability to convey the depth and complexity of Jung's work with such simplicity and heartfelt inspiration, empowering the feminine spirit. This book commands respect for its ability to reach the soul and guide readers toward true transformation.

I am confident that you, too, will find this book a source of profound insight and inspiration, just as I have. It is a work that not only enlightens the mind but also enriches the heart and soul.

Editor

Introduction

A Modern Ode to Ancient Wisdom

This book, "Awakening the Divine Feminine: The Pancha Prakṛiti Goddesses," is a heartfelt homage to the venerable tradition of the ancient rishis, whose sacred compositions have echoed through the ages. Building on profound hymns of Sri Suktam, Devi Suktam, Durga Suktam, and other ancient Vedic Stotras, this work seeks to weave the timeless wisdom of these ancient verses with the threads of contemporary life. Crafted in the style of our forebearers, this book is both a prayer to the divine and an offering to you, the reader. Each page, each chapter, mirrors the poetic elegance of the Suktams, designed to resonate with the soul's yearning for deeper spiritual connection.

As much as it is an expression of devotion, it is also a guide, intended to make the profound teachings of the Divine Feminine accessible and applicable in everyday situations. In the spirit of the Sanskrit compositions that have guided devotees for centuries, this book aspires to serve as a modern suktam to Devi—the Goddess. It is structured to be as potent and meaningful as the ancient texts, intended to enrich your spiritual journey and daily life with the grace and power of the goddesses it venerates.

As you turn these pages, may you find this ancient wisdom in a language that speaks directly to the heart, inviting the beauty of the Divine Feminine into your life, guiding, nurturing, and inspiring you to transcendence.

Author's Note

Dear seeker

In modern psychology, Carl Jung—in the West often considered far ahead of his time—stands as a genius and visionary whose insights into archetypes illuminate the universal patterns embedded within the human psyche. His work, revolutionary and deeply introspective, echoes with the timeless wisdom of the Eastern civilisations and spiritual traditions, where the awakening of archetypal energies has been a cornerstone of cultural and spiritual life for millennia.

This book weaves together these seemingly disparate threads—Jung's analytical approach to psychology and the poetic expression of the Ancient Rishis from the spiritual heritage of the East. Drawing from ancient scriptures such as the Suktams, Rig Veda, Upanishads plus extensive academic exploration of Jung's work, this book is crafted to engage heart, mind and spirit. It renders the intricate concepts of psychology through the evocative poetry of spirituality, reflecting the ancient texts, making the profound nature of archetypal energies both accessible and dynamic.

At the core of this exploration is Jung's concept of what he called the collective unconscious, a deep well of universal symbols and images, the matrix from which all human themes emerge. This book invites you, the reader, to interact with these archetypes—not simply as abstract concepts but as vibrant, living energies that can be engaged through devotion, ritual, and conscious action.

Aligned with the guiding spirit of our ancient Rishis, this book expands beyond the traditional practice of chanting, advocating for an active participation in the divine manifestation invoking the goddesses through a living experience. This is a call to transcend mere recitation and embody the profound wisdom of the divine feminine in our daily lives.

As you engage with these sacred teachings, you embark on a journey toward the powerful and compassionate blessings of the eternal, almighty, and most merciful Divine Mother. Through the timeless, Vedic poetic style, you create an inner space for receiving her divine grace. This method, tested through the ages, opens your heart to the profound and loving presence of the Divine Mother.

Author's Note

This work is crafted to be a companion, a transformational key inviting you to participate actively in the profound dance of the energies that shape our destinies. The book is designed to be read as a Vedic Suktam as part of your daily meditation practice and as an offering to the Divine Mother.

Love and Blessings

About the Author

Om Namo Bhagavate Vāsudevāya

Adi Kṛṣṇa Rama's spiritual journey began with his love for theoretical physics, driven by a profound curiosity about the universe's most elusive mysteries. Born with an insatiable hunger for knowledge, Adi Rama was captivated by the grand unified theory and the enigmatic forces of invisible matter and energy, which constitute over ninety percent of the cosmos. His quest for understanding took a dramatic turn when he began contemplating the singularity at the center of a black hole—a thought experiment that transformed his scientific inquiry into a profound spiritual journey.

From a young age, Adi K. Rama was known for his brilliance and determination. His peers and mentors recognized his exceptional intellect and boundless curiosity. As he delved deeper into the world of theoretical physics, his passion for uncovering the universe's secrets grew stronger. He was particularly fascinated by the idea of a grand unified theory, which promised to explain the fundamental forces of nature in a single framework. His research into the invisible components that dominate the cosmos, further fueled his drive to explore the unknown.

It was during a period of intense intellectual engagement that Adi K. Rama encountered a transformative moment. While grappling with the concept of a black hole's singularity, he experienced what he later described as his first satori—a sudden flash of enlightenment. This moment shattered the confines of his scientific understanding and opened the door to a new dimension of awareness. Adi K. Rama's journey had taken an unexpected turn, leading him away from purely intellectual pursuits and towards a profound spiritual awakening.

This newfound spiritual thirst led Adi K. Rama to explore the ancient wisdom of both Eastern and Western traditions. He immersed himself in sacred texts, philosophies, and the teachings of revered sages, embarking on a rigorous path of sadhana (spiritual practice). His spiritual journey was characterized by urgency, vitality, and unwavering devotion. This intense practice became the crucible for his transformation, a journey fueled by deep passion and an unyielding desire to encounter the divine infinite.

One silent morning, on a cremation ghat by a river, Adi K. Rama experienced a pivotal moment that would define his spiritual path. Near an old ashvattha tree, he stood on the edge of life and death, enveloped by a profound silence. In this stillness, he encountered the divine principle—the source of all energies. This experience defied the dualities of being and non-being, eluding full capture by both the Buddhist concept of shunyata (nothingness) and the Vedic notion of para Brahman (the infinite full of life). It was a revelation that, while indescribable, inspired endless reverence for its mystery.

Twenty-one years later, Adi Kṛṣṇa Rama began sharing his insights with the world through his books, talks and guidance.

Overview of the Book

Part One
The Pancha Prakṛiti Goddesses

Part 1 delves into the beauty and splendour of the pancha prakṛti; Ma Parashakti, Ma Saraswati, Ma Lakshmi, Ma Durga and Ma Kali, including the manifestations of Ma Lakshmi as Radha and Sita.

Ma Parashakti

Goddess of life, the creator, the infinite. Source of all energy. The chapter shows how to invoke Ma Prashakti in different ways, like through techniques that invoke life energy; pranayama, active meditations and connection with the vibrant energy of nature.

Ma Saraswati

Goddess of art, learning, wisdom, harmony, expression and longing for beauty. The chapter explores how to invoke the goddess within through cultivating curiosity, awe and wonder, pursuing with discipline and persistence, and learning skills for communication.

Ma Lakshmi

This chapter awakens the energy of Ma Lakshmi—abundance, wealth, fortune and family. It shows how to invoke the Goddess through working towards your vision and dreams, towards creating abundance and towards consciousness. It describes ways to to reach the goddess within through creating flow and stability as well as self care, gratitude and celebration.

Sita

Sita—the ultimate flowering of Ma Lakshmi as love and surrender. This chapter explores the manifestation of divine feminine as pure love, trust, devotion, loyalty, strength, patience, and feminine will and presence.

Radha

The greatest manifestation of divine feminine, the guidance to unconditional love. Her bhakti is the beacon for all seekers showing what surrender is, showing true leadership through the heart.

Ma Durga

This chapter invokes the powerful energy of Ma Durga, the embodiment of strength, power, and independence. It shows how to invoke the blessings of the goddess through the power of "no", through building good values and creating good systems, and when reaching power and strength fighting the demon of ego.

Ma Kali

This chapter stirs the energy of Mahakali—powerful, like a sword, with no compromises. Kali is urgency, change, and awakening. She reminds us to remember life as a gift and live every moment totally, urges us to bring awareness to consciousness, and commit fulheartedly to purpose, meaning and life.

Part Two
Questions to the Master

The second part of the book consist of questions from seekers on the path of inner transformation. Guruji answers the questions in a way that enables everyone on the spiritual path to benefit from the wisdom and guidance.

Radical Authenticity

Understand how to live authentically through commitment to honesty with yourself, looking inwards and finding out what you do not want, building a foundation of "no" before venturing into a fully committed "yes", and developing courage to stand with your authenticity and the expression of it.

Trusting in Life and Divine

In this chapter, we see how life has its own intelligence, and how the human mind takes life away from its intelligence and imposes its stupidity on it thereby losing the diamond of trust in life. Trust is the territory of the brave ones as it demands vulnerability, letting go of fears, seeing the wisdom of life and not seeing oneself outside of it.

Achieving True Happiness

Understand how happiness finds roots in meaning, and meaning can be sustained while happiness cannot. There is no set recipe for happiness, so celebrate life, and life will find joy and meaningful happiness.

From Problem Solving to Joy of Life

Experience the shift from problem solving to living a life of joy through seeing the absurdity, imperfections and meaningless of life. See how joy appears to a heart full of gratitude, a mind full of wonder and a spirit of rejoicing and celebrating.

The Power of Presence

Discover the importance of mastery of attention, and learn how to bring attention to the present moment through physical activity, flow of doing, fully awakened senses, and different meditation techniques.

Overcoming Problems in Meditation Practice

Learn how to overcome typical obstacles in meditation practices, master attention, avoid the pitfall of goal focus, and celebrate the individual journey of transformation.

Part Three
Guidance for Practices

The third part of the book provides practical guidance for different techniques mentioned in the book.

Vigyan Bhairav Tantra

This chapter explores the foundational meditation techniques of the ancient Book of Secrets. Guruji instructs the first 7 of the 112 techniques.

Pranayama

Pranayama breathing exercises awaken the prana energy, and through this chapter you will learn some of the most important pranayamas for cleansing and balancing the energy.

Osho Active Meditations

Osho's active meditation are designed for the modern seeker. This chapter gives instructions for some of the most popular of the techniques.

Beej Mantra

This short chapter explains the beej mantra and gives a beej mantra for each of the five goddesses.

Part One
THE PANCHA PRAKṚITI GODDESSES

Ma Parashakti

Ma Parashakti, Ma Ādyaśakti, Ma Parvati—from where all originates, where all will end. The infinite divine force from where all aspects of consciousness, of nature, of all and everything manifest. The divine, the ultimate supreme consciousness prevailing, the existence.

The powerhouse of infinite
The source of all energy
Ma Parashakti
She is the source
She is the divine

She is the divine manifestation. The divine manifestation from where life originates, the divine manifestation from where the nature arises. The divine manifestation from where all and everything originates. **The divine mother**. In our life, she is the source of all energies. She is the divine mother, the feminine, the nurturer, the nature. Mother in her nurturing, caring, and protecting. From where the motherhood originates.

Ādyaśakti, **where our senses find their origin**. She is the one who makes the eyes see, and the ears hear. She brings life to the touch. She gives feeling to the emotions, to empathy, to compassion. She gives compassion. From

where we get the ability to feel deeply, to see deeply, to hear, to know. From where knowingness comes, from where awareness comes, from where consciousness originates. She is the divine consciousness which gives life to our senses, which gives life to prana, which gives life to the body.

When you are conceived, it is the blessing of Ma Ādyaśakti, Ma Parashakti. When life starts to grow, it's the blessing of Ma Parashakti.

The movement, the flow of life
Life in itself
This moment is alive

We speak, we hear, we see this universe. We see the vastness of this universe. We feel the human emotions. We see light, we hear sound, we smell, we feel the touch. We can feel and sense. This is Ma Parashakti.

When we are aware how our attention, our emotions, our thoughts move, it's Ma Parashakti.

The power of love when in love
The power of silence
The power of is-ness
—Ma Parashakti.

She's the Ganga of life
She's the flow

She's the life which comes in the spring. She's the awakening which comes in the consciousness.

She's the movement which comes in the time.

She's the dance which comes with the music.

She's the beat. She's the rhythm.

When your heart beats, it's Ma Parashakti. It's her blessing.

When your breath moves
When you grasp for breath
When this moment comes alive
—Ma Parashakti

When she turns her face away from you
Everything stops, and death prevails
Nothing moves, everything comes to a halt
When she smiles, life moves
The beauty of Ma Parashakti

When there's love and devotion in your life
Magic appears, joy appears
—the blessings of Ma Parashakti.

Ma Parashakti

When your feet move in dance
With the spirit of life
—Ma Parashakti
When a song appears in your heart
—Ma Parashakti
When a smile is on your face
—Ma Parashakti
When nurtured, healed and loved
—Ma Parashakti
She's the divine blessing

When curiosity and wonder of the world
Find its spirit, find its meaning
—Ma Parashakti

She's the manifestation in the universe
The stars, the planets, the life forms
—Ma Parashakti

She's the guiding force
To awakening and enlightenment
She's the guiding force to joy
She's the love

When in the depth of the silence
She's vast, she's infinite

When you're born and have
Your first embrace of life
—Ma Parashakti

When you're conceived
Reaching the womb, the nurture
Where you grow and gather life
—Ma Parashakti.

When food becomes prana
—Ma Parashakti

When love blossoms
—Ma Parashakti
When inspiration shines
—Ma Parashakti
When joy kisses you
—Ma Parashakti

When your senses come alive
Full of life energy
Full of juice of life
Full of blessing of life
—Ma Parashakti

Ma Parashakti

When lush green spring
Fills you with vibrance
—Ma Parashakti

When seasons change from one to another
—Ma Parashakti

Cannot touch, cannot reach
If you try to bring her
From this mystery to life
You cannot find her
This is Ma Parashakti

The blessing which reaches you
The love which blossoms in your heart
The inspiration which comes from nowhere
The beauty that appears in a flower
The insight, the creative spark
The joy, the fulfilment, the peace

Mind however much it tries to understand it, define it, and encapsulate it, saying "this is", it cannot. The more I try to describe her, the more I lose words, and only a smile appears. The more I speak about her, only feelings remain. When Buddha was asked, "what is enlightenment?", only silence remained. All my life

I've been describing this mystical, vast, infinite force. Every time I feel that I cannot. This is the power of Ma Parashakti. She's there, yet you cannot reach. The mystical, the **mysterious consciousness** which appears in life.

How does a seed change to a flower?
How does winter change to spring?
How does night change to day?
How does a cloud become rain?

This is Ma Parashakti. From where all the manifestations come, from where all the creation appears, that's Ma Parashakti.

In yourself, reach Ma Parashakti. When you meet love in yourself, when gratitude, when joy, when the vital life force within you awakens, she will come to your life in many different forms.

When awareness meets attention, when awareness meets consciousness, when love meets freedom, Ma Parashakti is there.

When you stand in front of the river, when you hear the sounds of the river, Ma Parashakti is there.

When you stand in front of the vast majestic Himalayan

mountains, when you connect with the majestic beauty of life, Ma Parashakti is there.

When you see the starry sky, galaxies after galaxies, stars after stars, a mysterious night, Ma Parashakti is there.

When you hold your beloved in your arms, and feel contentment and love, Ma Parashakti is there.

When your senses come alive, throbbing with the ache of longing, when your heart opens, and tenderness and vulnerability flower, Ma Parashakti is there.

When your music finds its beats, its rhythm, Ma Parashakti is there.

When you sit in nurturing presence, when you feel nourished after a good meal, when the warmth of fire reaches you in the cold, when colors of spring surround you, Ma Parashakti is there.

When you find will in the most difficult times, Ma Parashakti is there.

The courage, the strength, the vitality
The presence, the silence, the being
The love, the blessings
The manifested, unmanifested, and yet to manifest
—Ma Parashakti.

When wisdom reaches your heart
—Ma Parashakti

When opportunities arise
—Ma Parashakti

Let Ma Parashakti's blessing reach you. Invoke the Shakti inside. Invoke the power of the feminine, the power of vital life force, the mother of all mothers. Such is the blessing of Ma Parashakti.

Stand under a waterfall and feel the life force inside.
Climb and cross the lake and feel the vitality inside.
Reach the heart of the forest and let prana reach the core of your being.
See the infinite sky and dissolve in the infinite nature of this existence.
Feel and melt in love.
Receive the divine blessing.
Receive the nurturing aspect of this universe.

Life is mysterious and mystical. How poetry reaches your heart, how art inspires you, how love finds way to your being, to your soul—this is mystery. How wisdom flowers, how the insights come, how creativity blossoms, how beauty comes in a flower and life moves from seed to flower—how that happens is a mystery of life. Don't try to understand it. Don't try to grasp it. Just a heart filled with love and trust. This is the devotion to Ma Parashakti.

Wherever you see life
Celebrate, acknowledge, be grateful
Respect life, celebrate life, rejoice life
Life in itself is Ma Parashakti
The magic of life, the magic called life

And let consciousness blossom
Like a thousand petal lotus
Let the longing to reach to your original self
To your divine infinite
She is love with Shiva, the divine
The vast infinite, the limitless infinite
She is the love of Shiva
She is free in his presence
She is the flow

And

When Shiva and Shakti meet
—Mahamudra happens
The highest of the high
The deepest of the deep
Oneness of consciousness
And the thousand petal lotus blossoms

Invoking Ma Parashakti

How to invoke Ma Adi Shakti's blessings in your life? Invoke the qualities Ma Adi Shakti cherishes.

The most important element when invoking Ma Shakti is **Prana**. See, feel, and know Prana. See Prana as the life energy moving in all dimensions of life, moving in every aspect of life. The ancient Taoists called it Chi. The ancient Shinto in Japan called it Kami, the spirit. The Vedics called it Prana. In the modern-day, we simply call it energy.

Invoke Ma Shakti by being aware of Prana, by invoking Prana. Prana can be invoked in multi-dimensional ways, from food, from good exercise, from yoga, meditation, sports, nature, daily rituals, invoking mantras, kirtan.

Dedicate time and attention during your day for Prana.

Spend time in nature. Live in harmony with nature, surrounded by nature. And if you live in city, then bring nature into the house. Take care of plants. India used to have a traditions of bringing Tulsi, holy basil into the house, a plant that represents Prana. Take care of Tulsi.

Bring all that invokes Prana into your life, like **nourishment from good food**. Take care of your food, growing your own food if possible. Have good meals with family and friends, filled with nourishment.

Practice **Pranayama**, especially cleansing Pranayamas like Kapalbhati and Bhasthrika and balancing pranayama like Bhramari Pranayama and Alom Vilom Pranayama[1].

For invoking Prana, learn **active meditations**. Learn different active meditations, especially Osho Active Meditations. Nothing invokes Prana in the modern-day world like Osho Active Meditations. Osho designed different Active Meditations for different times of the day, for example Kundalini Meditation, Dynamic Meditation, Nadbrahma, Guri Shankar, Mandala, Whirling Meditation. The Active Meditations involve a beginning stage of activity followed by a period of silence, accompanied by music designed for guiding though the different stages. They are available online[2].

Devote yourself to **Bhajan and Kirtan**. Bhajan and Kirtan are deeper and more subtle ways to invoke Mahashakti's energy in your heart.

---

1 See the section "Guidance for Practices" for instruction in these pranayamas.

2 See the section "Guidance for Practices" for overview of Osho Active Meditations

All goddesses derive their energy from Ma Parashakti. If you are not full of Prana, what energy could you give to invoke the qualities of the other goddesses in your life?

The core of all practices and activities invoking prana energy is the knack of **bringing awareness to the vibrance of life energy.** By shifting attention to this vibrance, a subtle awareness of life energy slowly starts developing in us. An intuitive intelligence of Prana, which is a blessing of Ma Parashakti, starts flowering, and a natural awareness of feelings and Prana becomes part of our life.

See how **different spaces have different energy**. When you organize your house, it changes the energy. When you change the interior of your house, it creates a different energy. Bring awareness to energy, bring awareness to Prana.

A good way to start being aware of the energies is by **spending time in nature**. Stand under a waterfall, go swimming in a lake. Connect with the nature. Allow the sunlight and the fresh air inside your house.

Bring awareness of prana to **love and devotion**. When you're in love or in devotion, you can feel a strong vibrance of energy. This vibrant energy, be aware of this energy, the change in energy.

Water is the physical form of prana on the Earth, and 60% of our body is water. So, remember to **drink water** during the day. Make it your daily rhythm to drink water and replenish your water with hydrating fruits and vegetables.

And the most important, **respect the feminine**, respect the woman. Nothing makes Ma Parashakti more angry than disrespect of the feminine, disrespect of the woman, disrespect of the woman inside and outside, of the feminine energy, of everything feminine in this universe. Since ages, women have been left aside by decision makers. The feminine view and expression is half the perspective of this existence, if not more, so learn from women with experience, and take advice from the feminine, especially before big decisions.

And **rejoice**. Rejoice the joy, the bubbling energy, the energy of life.

Respect the **inner youthfulness**, always. Stay young, with humor, with laughter.

Fall in love, follow your passion.

Learn to **understand different energies**. Learn feng shui, tai chi, chi qong, the ancient techniques of tantra. Read ancient scriptures.

And **connect to your senses**. When you're eating food, take time to pay attention to your food. Bring your senses to the food when you're eating. Rejoice and celebrate the senses. Don't escape from the senses. Bring awareness to the senses, bring consciousness.

Choose your life's journey, your hero journey. Make life an adventure, **rejoice life as an adventure**, as an exciting adventure. And see, isn't life wonderful? See the wonder of life. See the wonder of nature.

Spend time with **mother**, with mothers—the very mothering, nurturing energy. Respect mother nature and the mother in yourself, as Ma Shakti is Ma Anna Purna. Celebrate the qualities of compassion. Give time for healing, your inner and outer wounds in life. Nourish yourself. Ma Shakti is the mother of all mothers. Ma Shakti is the mother of all senses.

Connect with **the five elements**. Understand the nature of the five elements. Fire, water, earth, sky, air. Connect with your inner space through meditation. Connect with your inner fire through longing, through passion.

Connect with your inner water through flow, through spontaneity. Connect with your inner air through joy, through movement, through action, through prana. Connect with your inner earth through nourishment, through sleep, through good rest.

And **rejoice the vitality of life**. Bring vitality through nature, through active meditations, through love.

Travel and meet and connect with people.

Experience life in all its dimensions, as Ma Shakti is multi-dimensional. If you have the blessing of Ma Shakti, the blessing of life energy, she can manifest as Ma Lakshmi, as Ma Saraswati, as Ma Durga, as Ma Kali. So invoke Ma Shakti.

Learn Chakra Meditation, learn Bījamantra[3], learn Transcendental Meditation. It will give you subtle movement of energy. Be aware of movement of energy in all forms.

If meditation is too far for you, **connect with nature**. Go swimming. Go running in the nature. Go hiking. Go on long hikes. Live in the nature, connect with the nature. That in itself is an active meditation. You don't need any other meditation than that.

---

3 See the section "Guidance for Practices" for explanation of and guidance to Bījamantra

Learn to **take care of your body**. Exercising, stretching, massaging. Connect with different fragrances, essential oils.

Music. Put on music and dance. If you cannot do any of the other things, then give half an hour to music. Put on music and dance. Just dance to different music, completely out of your normal listening, a random playlist. Connect with drums. Drums invoke energy. Ma Adi Shakti loves the energy of the drums.

And learn to **move your attention**. Your attention should be free, not hooked by social media, by news, by gossip. If you can keep your attention free and stay master of your attention and awareness, you cut the bondages of Ma Adi Shakti inside you.

Cut all the bondages and free the inner Shakti through dance, through celebration, through joy, through love, through creativity.

Take a canvas and **paint**. If you do not know painting, just paint. Just go for colours and connect with the canvas.

Do something brave every day. A little thing away from your habits, out of your routine. Challenge yourself.

Remember, Ma Adi Shakti is infinite

When you feel that your energy is low and you are finishing the last of it, **the second wind will come**. I have seen that in mountaineering. After hours or days of walking, climbing high mountains, above 5000, 6000 meters, 7000 meters, when no energy is left, you take one more step, one more step, and a new wave of energy comes. So imagine Ma Adi Shakti as waves of the ocean. Have you ever seen waves of the ocean stopping or running out? Never.

She is infinite, remember, infinite

The way this universe is infinite, it's a reflection of Ma Adi Shakti because the universe is born from Ma Adi Shakti.

She gives birth
She is the mother of the universe
She is the Divine Goddess

Connect with people with simplicity of life and innocence of heart as Ma Shakti always blesses innocence and purity. Connect with open heart.

Respect the **wildness** inside, the raw, the wild. Never be scared of it as Ma Shakti is nature herself. Rejoice the wild and beautiful life-force of nature inside yourself.

Rejoice life, **celebrate life through sharing**. Sharing creates movement in life. Whatever you learn, share it. Whatever you have, give it. Whatever you seek, give it.

And gratefulness.

These are the qualities which invoke Ma Shakti. Pay attention to this whenever, wherever you can.

And once you have blessings of Ma Shakti, you will have the **inner space** for inviting Ma Lakshmi, Ma Saraswati, Ma Kali, Ma Durga. This inner space is made by Ma Shakti. So create that inner space to invite the other goddesses.

Let the feminine reach you, let Ma Shakti's blessing reach you in all dimensions.

Ma Saraswati

Ma Saraswati, the goddess of creativity and art, the goddess of knowledge and seeing, the goddess that brings the creation of this universe to light. The manifestation of all creativity in this universe is Ma Saraswati.

The beauty of purity and serenity, the **excellence** of wisdom. Wherever you see excellence, it's Ma Saraswati.

Wherever you find **art and creativity**, wherever you see creativity and art, expression of creativity in form of art, music, and culture, the beauty expressing itself as art and music, Ma Saraswati's blessing is there.

When you see books, when you see any **written word**, whether it is in form of technology or in printed form, Ma Saraswati is there.

When you see a desire, a **longing to learn**, to understand, to know, to follow the curiosity, when you have a deep respect for curiosity and the creative spark, Ma Saraswati is there. The blessing of Ma Saraswati is there.

When you see **harmony** in life, when you see balance, when you see harmony manifesting in different dimensions, when you see everything is flowing in a harmonious way, like in a well cooked and well served dish where all the spices are coming in a harmony, and

all the different ingredients are balancing each other, Ma Saraswati is there.

When there is **symphony** in the music, when all the instruments are playing in harmony, and the melodies are shaping into a beautiful form of art, Ma Saraswati's blessing is there.

When the beats are in a **rhythm** which is soothing to that moment or to that song or to that music, Ma Saraswati is there.

When you see your life, all different dimensions of life, falling into a harmonious flow, and there is an expression of inspiration and creativity and a spark of learning, of acquiring knowledge, and all your experiences are falling into wisdom, Ma Saraswati is there.

When you see your intelligence, your logic and reasoning crystallizing into **wisdom** which finds its expression, Ma Saraswati is there.

When you speak, and your words come into **harmony and beauty**, Ma Saraswati is there.

When **innovation** is coming in your life, when you are innovating, and you are becoming pioneer in your field, Ma Saraswati is there.

When you start to find **guidance towards the spiritual wisdom,** and you start to walk on the path where your Guru, your Master shows up, Ma Saraswati's blessing is there.

When your body is in a rhythm, in harmony, and the **health flows in the body**, in all the different parts of the body, functioning in harmony, Ma Saraswati is there.

So, wherever you see wisdom, art, creativity, purity, beauty, learning, curiosity, harmony, balance, and wisdom, Ma Saraswati is there.

When you start to **express yourself**, your feelings and your emotions and your thoughts and different dimensions of your being, whether through words, spoken word, written word, through art, or through music, Ma Saraswati is there.

Wherever in the universe there is a **spark of creativity**, in the form of spring, when the flower blossoms, when the bud opens, when the flower comes out from the bud, Ma Saraswati is there.

Om Saraswati Namah
Om Saraswati Namah

She is a beautiful beacon of wisdom. She is a river of creativity. She is the soil in which knowledge find its roots in its purest form. She is the manifestation of divine in the symbol of intellectual, artistic pursuits in form of wisdom, in form of intelligence, guiding us towards the light of insight, understanding and the harmony of expression, form of self-expression, in form of feelings.

The Goddess Saraswati, Ma Saraswati. The purity, tranquility, peace. Riding upon a swan, a symbol of elegance, sitting upon a lotus, the symbol of beauty, purity and the clarity which comes when we are able to see things without any illusion. Ma Saraswati's blessings are the roots.

When the path to enlightenment becomes clearer and clearer, when there is **inner peace**, and simplicity starts to manifest in the life, Ma Saraswati's blessing is there.

When the spirit of intellect, awareness, and different forms of intelligence, all is coming into harmony, into wisdom, Ma Saraswati's blessing is there. This is the beauty of Ma Saraswati.

In the East, she has always been inspiring artists. Musicians have always been worshipping her, seeking her blessing, reaching out to her. As an archetype, she represents immense curiosity, immense creativity, and a **rebellious spirit towards creativity**. A rebellious spirit not towards transcendence, but towards expression as creativity and the transcendence which comes from the creative expression, the creative expression of life. Whenever and wherever there is creative expression of life, the archetype of Ma Saraswati, or the divine energy of Ma Saraswati as one would say in the East, wakes up.

And through that blessing, in that blessing, **joy**, which is deeply rooted in the pursuit of creativity, starts to blossom in the pursuit of knowledge, in the pursuit of artistic expression.

When music reaches the hearts of people, when art in its best form inspires a whole generation, the divine energy of Ma Saraswati comes alive.

In the feminine expression, she represents immense respect, immense dedication, and immense devotion to knowledge, to intelligence, to wisdom, to creativity, to art, to music, to expression. And not only expression, but preserving the expression, whether it is in form of words, whether it is form of music, whether it is in form of visuals.

And when we find **inspiration of creative expression**, Ma Saraswati's blessing has reached us.

When we pursue the hardship of mastering a music instrument, that is a prayer to Ma Saraswati.

When we work on an intellectual problem that is very difficult to solve, and we dedicate ourself in the pursuit of it, that is a prayer to Ma Saraswati invoking the archetype in our deep consciousness of Ma Saraswati.

To invoke this divine energy of Ma Saraswati, we **dedicate ourselves in the pursuit of knowledge**, **of wisdom, of art, of mastery**, we are offering prayers to Ma Saraswati.

And when we offer prayers, when we invoke the dimension of Ma Saraswati, she is coming to bless you. She would be there, invoked, she would be there manifesting from deep within in your consciousness.

So, dedicate yourself with discipline, dedicate yourself with dedication, with complete dedication filled with perseverance, with a consistent practice, a deep sense of commitment towards the **pursuit of learning**. A learning which is not only in order to reach a goal of clearing a test or an exam—that is not the way you offer prayers to Ma Saraswati. You offer prayers to Ma Saraswati when you are dedicated to the pursuit of learning.

The same is for music instruments. When your goal is to practice your instrument in order to create a song or reach out to your audience, that is fine. But the prayer you offer to the divine energy of Ma Saraswati will be when you dedicate yourself in devotion to your music instrument or the process of creating music, then you are praying in devotion to Ma Saraswati, and that is your offering, that is your divine offering to Ma Saraswati.

In the love for pursuit of knowledge, in the love for mastery, in the love of wisdom, in the love of creativity, in the love of art for the sake of art, creativity for the sake of creativity, when in this process you get in the **zone where the time disappears**, where the space disappears, where there is nothing left and only creativity prevails, Ma Saraswati manifests.

So, **the prayer starts with dedication**, the prayer starts with devotion, the prayer starts with consistent perseverance in pursuit of learning, developing a creative spark, developing a sense of curiosity and wonder in yourself, a sense of imagination.

When you **sharpen your intellect**, when you bring your life experiences together into crystallization from which wisdom will take birth, this gives a new dimension to your life. This gives a new dimension.

I invite you to this divine prayer
To Ma Saraswati
To this transformative journey
This journey towards awakening
Awakening of life
Awakening of creativity
Awakening of deep inner peace
Awakening of wisdom
Awakening of art
Awakening of music and learning
Within yourself

Ma Saraswati's presence is like the soothing moonlight illuminating our path and illuminating the paths of artists, scholars, seekers, illuminating the path of innovators and pioneers.

In this world which is full of noise and distraction, Ma Saraswati invites us to **dive deep into the ocean of wisdom**, ocean of knowledge, to seek the pearls of wisdom that lie beneath the surface of this endless chaos in the world.

Today the world is full of unnecessary time wasting on the idiot box called TV, on your devices, on your phones. Ma Saraswati's invitation to you is to **the**

world of wonder. Ma Saraswati's invitation to you is in the world of curiosity, in the world of passion. A passion for learning, a passion for wisdom, a passion for inviting the longing which takes us to divine, giving us opportunity to grow and evolve and eventually evolving our consciousness, eventually evolving as transcendence within us.

There is an ancient saying in India, "**invite Ma Saraswati into your life and all her sisters will follow**". And that's how it is. It has always been like that. If you go and pray to Ma Lakshmi for abundance and wealth, it is very difficult, but if you go to Ma Saraswati and pray through your dedication to learning, through your dedication to pursuit of knowledge, pursuit of creativity, pursuit of inspiration, she will invite Ma Lakshmi in your life, she will invite abundance. She will invite Ma Durga, the power, the strength, the independence. She will invite Ma Shakti, the nurture, the nourishment, the health, the transcendence. She will invite the total transformation of Ma Kali because you would have all the opportunities for bringing transcendence in your life.

So, pursue knowledge, pursue art, pursue creativity. And pursue it with **dedication**. That dedication is the prayer to Ma Saraswati, that dedication is the prayer to Ma Saraswati. The perseverance on the path is the prayer to Ma Saraswati.

Ma Saraswati holds a veena, a symbol of harmony of all life's aspects, reminding us that **creativity is the soul song**, the song of the deepest core of our consciousness, and each one of us is born with a unique melody to share with the world. Your unique talent, your unique skills, your unique expression, your unique inspiration. Seek and Ma Saraswati would be the happiest.

Be authentic to yourself. Find your unique talent, your unique skill, your unique expression, and Ma Saraswati's blessing would be bestowed upon you. Stay true to yourself, don't get inspired by ideas imposed upon you. Your father wanted you to be engineer or this or that. All that is good, but finding your unique expression would be a prayer to Ma Saraswati, finding your unique abilities would be an offering to Ma Saraswati, and then dedicating yourself in the pursuit would be a prayer with roots in your hard work, a prayer that's not just spoken words, some repeated mantra, but with roots in your sweat, blood and tears. And when you pray with your sweat, blood and tears to the divine goddess of art and creativity, magic is bound to shine in your life, magic is bound to come in your life from all dimensions in form of harmony, in form of creativity, in form of inspiration.

She inspires you to **unleash your creative potential** whether it is through painting, through writing, through dancing, or through any other expression. And when you express your feelings and emotions, Ma Saraswati's blessings reach the core of your being. This expression can reach to its pinnacle through poetry, through dance, through music.

The balance which comes when we see the **interconnectedness of all things**, how the whole nature, the whole existence is interconnected. When we see this and respect it, we offer prayers to Ma Saraswati, and the divine energies of Ma Saraswati start to wake up in our consciousness, start to shine, start to be reflected in different aspects of our life, expressing themselves in form of grace, in form of dignity, in form of elegance.

See how Ma Saraswati sits with her Veena and her white clothes—**such elegance, such integrity, such dignity**. And when this dignity, integrity and grace manifests, all the energies go even deeper and invoke compassion in us. And when compassion starts to transform, when your art, your knowledge, your creativity serves humanity through your expression of compassion or it becomes the expression of compassion, you offer a great divine prayer to Ma Saraswati, and she's the happiest.

All the dimensions of knowledge go to the deep expression or **flowering of compassion.** The knowledge and pursuit not just serving your interests but serving the interest of the humanity, of the whole of the planet, of others. When your art serves humanity and inspires generations, when your technological innovations reach the world and make the world a better place, when your knowledge starts to transform the lives of others, when your wisdom starts to reach the world and changes lives—that is the greatest prayer you can offer to Ma Saraswati.

When the Wright brothers dreamt of giving wings to humanity and taking the humanity forward, they offered great prayers to Ma Saraswati. When a scientist discovered penicillin and cured many illnesses for generations to come, that was an offering to Ma Saraswati. When your music reaches the soul of people, bringing inspiration, peace, and joy into their lives, Ma Saraswati is happy. When your wisdom transforms and transcends the lives of others, Ma Saraswati is happy.

May you invoke the great divine energies of Ma Saraswati in your consciousness. May you invoke this wonderful feminine archetype inside. May you pay deep respect to this expression through which our whole creation came to existence. It is through the blessings of Ma Saraswati that the whole creation came to existence.

Wherever symphony and harmony comes in the music, it's Ma Saraswati.

When all the cells in our body start to function in a harmonious way, it's Ma Saraswati.

When your emotions and feelings come into harmony in form of joy, it's Ma Saraswati.

When all the different aspects of your body falls into harmony, and the harmony becomes health, it's Ma Saraswati.

When all your thoughts fall into harmonious expression and intelligence comes, it's Ma Saraswati.

When all the wisdom from your experiences in life become crystallised as deeper wisdom, Ma Saraswati.

When all your insights form into clarity, Ma Sarawati.

When the great awakening revolutionises your consciousness and enlightenment prevails, Ma Saraswati manifests.

May you be blessed with the devotion of Ma Saraswati, the great goddess Saraswati.

Invoking Ma Sarawati

How to invoke Saraswati in your life? What should one do, how should one live to invoke the blessings of Mahasaraswati?

The most important element, which is the greatest offering to Mahasaraswati, is having a sense of awe, **a sense of wonder**. There is a story of Newton and his nephew. Once Newton was having a walk with his nephew. His nephew saw an apple fall from a tree, and he asked his uncle, "uncle Newton, if the apple falls, does that big apple, the moon in the sky, also fall?" Now, this is a sense of wonder. With this sense of wonder, the whole science of physics emerged, all that we have available today.

So, **start with wonder**, start with curiosity. See what gives you that sense of awe and sense of wonder, whether you receive that sense of wonder in form of curiosity or when you see a beautiful flower you feel like, "oh wow". The sense of "wow", the sense of awe, the sense of "how?", all these feelings invoke Mahasaraswati inside, invoke her blessings inside. The moment you feel this "wow!", "how?", "why?"—this curiosity, wanting to learn, fascination, you invoke Mahasaraswati inside.

When we have curiosity, when we have wonder, when we have awe, those feelings reach Mahasaraswati directly. Those feelings reach her.

Pursue these feelings of awe, wonder and curiosity. Don't just stop there, waiting for someone to tell you. Seek, search. If you have a question, go to a library. These days Google is available, and we can search on Google, but learning through Google it not such an in-depth process. For learning, books are still one of the best ways. Find a book, search for a book, study, learn. And when you start learning, when you start to follow your curiosity, follow your question, when you start to ask, you have already begun the journey with Mahasaraswati. You are already her devotee. You are on the path, and she has started to guide you.

And when you get into the **habit of following your curiosity and pursuing it**, that's when the real learning begins.

Learning is not when it is imposed upon you and you have to. True learning comes from curiosity, a sense of wonder, a sense of enquiry. So, pay attention to these feelings inside. Whenever you have this emotion, this feeling, this sense of wonder and enquiry, looking into things with curiosity, that's where Mahasaraswati resides. Mahasaraswati is in the feeling, in curiosity, in wonder—this is her abode.

And when you start to **pursue it with discipline**, start showing up every day at the library with your book, or showing up with the thing you are learning. If you are learning an art form, like learning music, every day begin at the same time. Have a six o'clock time decided that "this is the time I will practice my music". Show up at six o'clock, day after day after day. This is the best prayer you can offer to Mahasaraswati, discipline. And when you have this persistent perseverance dedicated to your process of learning, Mahasaraswati's light starts reaching you, Mahasaraswati's blessing starts nurturing you.

Mahasaraswati's blessing is very subtle, you may not notice it. When you practice a music instrument, you trust, and you show up day after day after day, and eventually in one year time, in two years time, when the results come, you will be surprised how powerful they are. But in the process, you need to trust in your discipline, in your practice, in your perseverance, in your consistency—day after day. This is the best prayer to Mahasaraswati, showing up consistently, persistently, day after day, in your sense of wonder, in your sense of awe. We wait for inspiration to come, but Mahasaraswati blesses those who offer her the flower of discipline, the flower of consistent, persistent action.

Now there are times of the day when Mahasaraswati's blessing is at the peak. Early morning, four to seven o'clock. Wake up early morning, and start the process of learning, reading, whatever art and knack you are learning, start early morning, that's the time when Mahasaraswati's blessing is at the peak because **she's subtle**, and this time is the most subtle. The light is subtle, the air is fresh, and the light is yet to come, it's neither day nor night, that is the time you meet Mahasaraswati. Or when the momentum is at its peak, you are learning, learning, learning, learning, and you take the day into the night, in this peak of momentum, you will meet Mahasaraswati.

Mahasaraswati deeply appreciates the **deep longing for beauty.** When you hear beautiful music, good rhythms, good melody, good composition, and you fall in love with it, you love it, you are admiring it, you are appreciating it, you are spending time in the joy of the music, of the beauty.

Spend time with people who have gained **mastery**

of their insights, of their skills. One of my favourite internet platforms is Masterclass, that's the place I see the blessings of Mahasaraswati, where people who have mastered their skill, that art form, that learning process to its peak, they are sharing it. Imagine the journey they have taken to reach to this mastery , years of years, and now they are sharing it. That is the place where you receive blessings of Mahasaraswati.

At home, make it cozy. There is a Danish word called "hygge" or "hyggelig". Create hyggelig spaces where you can sit and reflect on life, where you can dedicate time to reading, to learning, to thinking, to writing. Make sure that you have that space in your house. In old times when the houses were more thoughtful, there was a room for studying. These days that is missing from the houses, **a room dedicated to Mahasaraswati**. Make a room dedicated to Mahasaraswati. Put a yoga mat there, put a meditation mat there, put music instruments there, put a veena there, put your reading, or your writing. You can have your computer there, but not your mobile phone. Your computer if it is dedicated to learning. Make the room inspiring with art, with paintings. Or if you do not have that much space, make a corner in your house. Make a space, a center in your house, dedicated to learning, dedicated to beauty, dedicated to art. This is the best offering you can give to Mahasaraswati. And when you give this offering, bring the image of Mahasaraswati. Hang a painting of Mahasaraswati there and chant Mahasaraswati's mantra with offerings of flowers and incense. Have music in the room, and play all the music you love. Surround yourself with art, music, books.

This is the outer. For the inner, curiosity, wonder, awe, and dedication to learning.

Organize your thoughts through writing. Nothing organizes thoughts like writing does. Write points, stories, insights—write, create. When you communicate through the written word, it's a totally different kind of communication. If reading is one step, then writing is the other step, and they go hand in hand, they go one after the other.

Learn communication, learn speaking, learn a new language. If that doesn't interest you, then master your own language, learn new words. If that doesn't interest you either, bring rhythm to your language, express emotions and feelings. In this way you make a path that reaches Mahasaraswati.

And **find a mentor**. The tradition of mentor and mentee has disappeared, the Guru Shishya Parampara. Find your Guru. Find a mentor who teaches you a specific skill, a specific art. If you are blessed with meeting your spiritual Guru, you truly are a blessed one.

And when you have awe, wonder, curiosity in questioning, and you have discipline to learn music, art, when you express, speak, and put your words right, when you paint, when you are sculpting, when you have mentor, when you have your Guru and you are learning day after day—Mahasaraswati reaches you.

Then dedicate your time to meditation. **Learn to meditate.** Give your time to meditation. Before you start something, take a break and be watchful. Pay attention.

When you do this, all of this or some of it, day after day, month after month, week after week, year after year—Mahasaraswati reaches you. You reach Mahasaraswati. She starts to blossoming inside you. Her blessings start to flow.

And when Mahasaraswati comes, she invites all her sisters because she is harmony. She is connected to all her sisters. She is the one who brings harmony to all. When you find harmony in your life, Mahasaraswati is there. When you find a good balance in your life,

Mahasaraswati is there. **Seek balance, seek harmony**. The blessings of all the sisters of Mahasaraswati will reach you. Invoke Mahasaraswati, and all the goddesses will bless you, will reach to you.

Such is the blessing of Mahasaraswati
Such is the blessing of the Divine Mother
Of serenity, of peace, of knowledge, of art
Of creativity, of wonder, of awe, of learning
Of discipline, of persistence, of the process of creation
Such is Ma Saraswati

Let her music compose
Let her insights give you clarity
Let her discipline give you strength
Let her serenity reach your heart and bring peace

And let her blessings make way for the blessings of Mahalakshmi, Ma Durga, Ma Parashakti, and Ma Kali.

Ma Lakshmi

Goddess Lakshmi, goddess of wealth, prosperity, abundance, fortune, and a multidimensional expansion in life. Goddess of divine abundance, of abundance on many different levels, goddess of prosperity on many different levels, whether it is the wealth in form of health, or wealth in form of success, wealth in form of prosperity, or wealth in form of influence. Goddess Lakshmi's blessing is there.

The archetype of Goddess Lakshmi, as we would understand it in the West, is the **archetype of abundance.** The archetype of abundance in form of harvest, abundance in form of nature, in form of flowers, spring, abundance in form of spring. That is a beautiful expression of Mahalakshmi in the nature. Abundance in form of a good monsoon rain in India, in form of a climate and weather supporting the harvest.

In our life the **feeling of abundance**, the feeling of joy, enjoying the life, celebrating the life, rejoicing the life.

What is **abundance in the body**? Abundance in the body is health and vitality and vigour, and the senses celebrating it, the senses rejoicing it, the senses reaching vigour and rejoicing and celebrating the vitality. And there is a balance in this vitality, this health, and the

senses are rejoicing this vitality. This is manifestation of Mahalakshmi in our body.

What would be manifestation of **Mahalakshmi in our mind**? A sense of expansion, of multi-dimensional growth, not feeling limited by our circumstances, not feeling limited by the situations we are in, but believing in ourself and visioning, dreaming and celebrating our vision, celebrating our life, flowing and moving towards our dreams. Celebrating our desires, seeing them and recognizing them, being aware of our desires, our longings, our wantings, our needs. Acknowledging it, recognizing it, knowing it. This is manifestation of Mahalakshmi in our mind.

Manifestation of **Mahalakshmi in our heart** is celebration of love, abundance of meaning, abundance of purpose. A meaningful deep relation, growing deeper every day, every year, every month, expanding, discovering new horizons. A healthy family, a happy and joyous family, a deep connection with the family, being rooted in the family.

Manifestation of **Mahalakshmi in the world** is prosperity. She is wealth and abundance in the world, in your life, blessing you with deep-rooted financial stability and success, ensuring that your material needs are always fulfilled, and you have freedom of action and are not limited by money or lack of resources, lack of network, lack of influence. She's making sure that you have all it requires. Whether you would like to pursue an education, whether you would like to pursue your dreams, or whether you would like to pursue your success, her blessings will make sure that you move in that direction.

With her blessings, the heart develops **generosity** and a deep-rooted **kindness**, encouraging sharing of wealth in a meaningful way, sharing resources in a meaningful way, building a strong sense of friendship and community and sense of belonging.

Sitting on a lotus with the expression of abundance and wealth around her, she represents **flowering of consciousness**. It's not only in wealth and abundance the consciousness flowers. With the blessing of Mahalaksmi, your spiritual pursuits start to get fulfilled, or you have opportunity for your spiritual pursuits to get fulfilled.

And from Malakshmi's blessing, **beauty** manifests. She's beautiful. Beautiful on many different levels. There is a **beauty in freedom**. When you see beauty in freedom, you have the blessing of Malakshmi. When you see a curse in poverty, you have started to receive the blessings of Malakshmi. When the pain of the limitation, the bondage of poverty hits you, that's the time you are worshipping Malakshmi.

What makes Ma Lakshmi happy? Rejoicing. **Rejoicing her blessings with gratitude** in your heart for what you have in your life. When you celebrate that, when you rejoice that, when you bring gratefulness to that, Ma Lakshmi is happy. When you see your skills, when you see your talents, when you see your abilities, when you see your haves, when you bring attention to that and feel the deep sense of gratitude and the deep sense of generosity, Ma Lakshmi is happy. If you have a good family, feeling the sense of meaning in the family—this is a prayer to Ma Lakshmi. Spending meaningful time with your family is a prayer to Ma Lakshmi. If you have good health, then celebrate your health, recognize the health and be thankful for it. You might be on the death bed, but be grateful for those last breaths, because you have breathing, you're alive, you're alive. Whatever moments are left in your life, they're still there. That gratitude, that deep sense of gratitude, that deep sense of love is the blessing, and your gratitude for this is the prayer, is the worship. When you celebrate and rejoice abundance, when you're not envious of the abundance of others but rejoicing it, when you get inspired by the success of others instead of feeling lack, when you pay attention to your needs and make sure that to fulfil them instead of complaining about them not being fulfilled—this is a prayer that reaches Ma Lakshmi.

When you **work towards creating abundance**, when you recognize abundance, when you pay attention to where abundance is, where wealth is, where resources are, where your inner resources are, your abilities, your talents, your skills, your hard work, your vision, your education, then you see where the resources are in the world. So, start with gratitude, start with paying attention to what you have in your life.

Then **visioning where your journey goes**, visioning the blossoming of the lotus of abundance in your life.

And from there—**courage, strength and will**. Persistent, consistent in the direction of abundance, in the direction of your vision, of your dreams—this is the prayer, this is the worship that reaches Ma Lakshmi.

She goes to the brave ones, she goes towards strength. Malakshmi is attracted to **vision**. Her husband—consciousness—is vision, expansion, infinite consciousness. Courage is vision, strength is vision. Malakshmi is at the feet of vision, lying in the ocean of abundance, lying in the ocean of creation. She's devoted to strength, to courage. She's devoted to vision. She's devoted to consciousness, to the infinite consciousness, and in the infinite consciousness she flows.

To seek the blessing of Ma Lakshmi, **seek strength**, work towards strength, work towards courage, towards vision, towards abundance, towards consciousness, towards flowering of the consciousness. Ma Lakshmi's blessing would be bestowed upon you because she seeks these qualities. Through this, spiritual wealth will start to flower in your life, not only material wealth—that's the foundation which is bound to happen. It is spiritual wealth which nurtures your soul, which invokes awakening, which guides you towards fully flowered enlightenment. So, with brave heart seek abundance, with brave heart work towards strength, with brave heart seek freedom and follow your dreams. Walk towards your vision.

Celebrate your life, have gratitude. See your abilities and resources, see your talents, put them into practice and master them.

See yourself in the presence of Vishnu. See yourself at the feet of Vishnu. Vishnu represents the vastness of the manifested and unmanifested existence. Malakshmi's blessing would be with you. Abundance will flow towards you, freedom will be beautifully manifesting in your life, and consciousness will blossom in form of love, in form of beauty, in form of harmony, in form of balance. Such is the blessing of Mother Lakshmi, Mother Lakshmi, Mother Lakshmi.

May Mother Lakshmi nurture your life
May she nurture multi-dimensional expansion
Multi-dimensional growth
Multi-dimensional abundance
May you celebrate life with gratitude
May you rejoice life with joy and beauty
May beauty be expressed in every aspect of your life
May vitality and vigour reach the deepest core
Of your being, of your prana, of your health
May Mother Lakshmi manifest
As an abundance of prana
An abundance of life energy

When you feel your life energy reaching to its peak, that's Mother Lakshmi's blessing.

When you feel youthfulness inside, when you feel joy, when you feel inspiration, when you feel full of life, Mother Lakshmi's blessing is with you.

Ma Lakshmi

When your life is full of freedom and vitality and vigour, and you celebrate, and you are grateful, Mother Lakshmi's blessing is with you.

When you vision, and you courageously walk towards your vision, when you dream, and you believe in your dream, Mother Lakshmi's blessing is with you.

When you connect with the nature and celebrate Mother Lakshmi's expression in form of nature, Mother Lakshmi's blessing reaches you.

When love finds meaning and joy, Mother Lakshmi's blessing reaches you.

May this abundance reach
The deepest core of your heart
The deepest core of your being
The deepest core of your life
May it expand as Vishnu expands
In all dimensions of life to the infinite
Because in the infinite, Mother Lakshmi resides
At the feet of infinite, Mother Lakshmi rests
Mother Lakshmi finds peace and love and harmony
May such be your life.

Invoking Mahalakshmi

Everybody would love to receive the blessings of Mahalakshmi. She reaches you through Mahasaraswati, so seek the blessings of Mahasaraswati, and she will call Mahalakshmi to you.

But let's see how you can devote yourself to Mahalakshmi, how you can bring the blessings of Mahalakshmi into your life.

What does Mahalakshmi love the most? She loves flow. She loves abundance. She loves stability. She loves flow of connections, emotions, feelings. She loves experiences. She loves fortune. So invoke these qualities in your life.

Create flow. When you make your house, make it so there is a flow of air, flow of energy, flow of movement. Curves, movements.

Mahalakshmi is goddess of **gratitude**. When you deeply feel great gratitude, when you are deeply appreciating life, Mahalakshmi's blessing reaches you. Write down what you are grateful for. Keep a gratitude diary. Make a place where you put all the pictures of what you are grateful for or write it as a story in your diary, so your attention goes to all the places in your life you are grateful for. Even tiny things. Light, water, a flower. Visualize everything you are grateful for and say "thank you, thank you, thank you". Gratitude is the greatest offering you can give. And this offering of gratitude to Mahalakshmi is the greatest. Mahalakshmi feels gratitude. Your gratefulness reaches, so offer your gratitude. See everything you are grateful for in your life. Write it down, put it on a vision board, surround yourself with it.

And Mahalakshmi loves spring. She loves **abundance in form of spring**. Put fruits and flowers in your house. Make a place for flowers, and nurture and take care of the flowers. Surround yourself with abundance. Wherever you live, whether you live in a big, wonderful, well-designed house or a small hut, bring flowers. You can make a small hut full of abundance with flowers, with fragrance. So make your space abundant. Get inspiration from spring. Spring is Mahalakshmi.

The way meaning is to Ma Saraswati, the same way gratitude and abundance is to Mahalakshmi.

And **take good care of yourself**, of your body. Mahalakshmi deeply appreciates it. Mahalakshmi loves care. She's goddess of self-care. Buy yourself nice clothes. Take good care of yourself. When you love your body the way it is, when you take good care of your body, when you take good care of your heart, your mind, Mahalakshmi's blessing reaches you.

She's also goddess of shringar—beauty and its expression.

Mahalakshmi, the divine embodiment of abundance, loves the essence of **flow**. She whispers to us through the movement in our lives. To honor her, embrace the fluidity that she cherishes.

Begin with the simple acts: if you do not possess a driving license, attain one. Feel the freedom of the open road. If your heart finds joy in walking, let your feet traverse the trails of nature, immersing yourself in the rhythmic dance of hiking.

In the realm of trade and commerce, witness the dynamic energy of wealth as it flows. Mahalakshmi's presence is felt in the circulation of money, a tangible form of her divine essence.

Spend time with your loved ones, for Mahalakshmi resides in the warmth of family bonds. Observe the vibrant flow of life during festivals like Divali and Holi, or in the West, during Christmas. Families gather, light illuminates the darkness, and celebration fills the air. This is the sacred dance of Mahalakshmi.

Embrace movement in all aspects of life, for through this, you invite the grace of Mahalakshmi into your heart and home.

Mahalakshmi loves **celebration**. She loves celebrating life. Create the joy of celebration in your life. Bring your family together, celebrate events, birthdays, special occasions. Find excuses for celebration.

Mahalakshmi graces us with the power of visualization. She is the weaver of dreams, urging us to dream boldly. Let not fear cloud your dreams. Envision your life with clarity and purpose. Mahalakshmi is the harbinger of desire. Do not shrink from your desires, but embrace them. Write down your deepest wishes, for she is the goddess of dreams, desires, and wishes. Dream, desire, and visualize, for in this, you invoke the blessings of Mahalakshmi, enriching your life with her divine presence.

Immerse yourself in life stories, for Mahalakshmi is also the goddess of **stories**. Through narratives, we connect with the essence of life and the universe. Let stories guide you, inspire you, and fill your heart with boundless possibilities.

And stay true to **fortune**, to luck. Happy go lucky, the right place at the right time. Aim for the best. It's very interesting how some of the best companies were started in Harvard and Stanford and other places where fortunes are made. Aim for fortune.

Aim for places where there is **wealth**. Wealth of knowledge, wealth of nature, wealth of spirituality, wealth of success, and most importantly wealth of health, wisdom, joy, compassion, and love .

Mahalakshmi is also goddess of **experiences**. In the same way Mahasaraswati is goddess of meaning, fulfillment, and peace, Mahalakshmi is goddess of experiences. Experience life, travel, listen to new music, try different types of food, meet people, read, watch movies. Experience.

Mahalakshmi, the divine goddess, is the embodiment of **stability**. To honor her, cultivate stability in your life. Build your home, secure your land, for she is the goddess of foundation and security.

She blesses the harvest, and through her, we learn the importance of **preparing and organizing**. Arrange your kitchen meticulously, so you need not constantly seek the fleeting joy of supermarket shopping. Create a well-stocked storage, ensuring you have what you need at hand.

Through stability and preparation, you invite Mahalakshmi's blessings into your life, grounding yourself in her divine grace. Embrace the steadiness she offers, and let your life flourish with her abundant blessings.

Mahalakshmi, the goddess of abundance, invites us to embrace her boundless blessings. Do not limit this abundance to mere money and wealth, but let your life overflow with abundance in all forms. Let your kitchen be a haven of plenty with a bounty of fruits, flowers, and nourishing healthy food. By embracing abundance in all its forms, you invite the grace of Mahalakshmi into your life, enriching it with her divine presence.

Mahalakshmi is also goddess of **celebration of the family space**. Cherish your family, bringing them together in harmony. Create spaces that foster togetherness—a welcoming, warm, and inviting home. Design these spaces to nurture and celebrate the bonds of family.

Mahalakshmi is goddess of **money**. Create different income streams in your life. Passive income, active income. Learn entrepreneurship, learn investment, learn trading. Build a company because in the company there's a flow. There's a flow of ideas. There's a flow of people. There's a flow of money. Create that flow.

When you offer these qualities in your life to Mahalakshmi, her blessings will reach you.

Mahalakshmi is goddess of **legacy and inheritance**. Take care of your inheritance, and if you don't have any, start building an inheritance for your children. Leave a legacy for the next generation. Make a company for the next generation. Build it and make it flower so you can pass it on. Have savings so you can give it.

Mahalakshmi is also goddess of **good deeds,** of sharing, of donation. Honour her through donating, giving to a cause, or volunteering.

When you imagine Mahalakshmi
Imagine spring, abundance, harvest
Imagine a flow of rivers, of rain
A flow of joy, of celebration

Life is a celebration
Life is a song
Life is tears of gratitude

Let Mahalakshmi flow to you
And through you reach beauty and consciousness
For humanity, for the next generation
For goodness, for Satyam Shivam Sundaram

When through you, Mahalakshmi reaches
Satyam Shivam Sundaram
Sat Chit Anand
This is a great blessing
Be that vessel, be that open heart
For Mahalakshmi to reach you

When Mahalakshmi manifests like this in your life, from there she will manifest as Sita, as Radha, as devotion and surrender. That's the flowering, that's the blossoming, that's the spring. In the same way Ma Saraswati comes to flowering through excellence, mastery, creation, harmony and balance, Mahalakshmi comes **to flowering as devotion, as surrender**, as Sita and Radha. This is the ultimate flowering of Mahalakshmi, when the heart leads, when devotion leads, when love leads, when surrender leads, when beauty leads.

May you have the blessing of Mahalakshmi, and may you reach the ultimate flowering of Mahalakshmi as manifestation of Sita and Radha.

Ma Sita

Sita, who is Sita? The Goddess Sita. Who is Sita Ma, the great queen? Sita Rama. When you say Rama, you say Sita Rama. Who is Sita? Daughter of great king Janak. Very few know how she came to this world. Sita was found by Janak, under the earth, when he was ploughing land. His plough hit a box. How did Sita reach there? Nobody knows the story of that. To the heart of Janak, she was the greatest gift ever received. He took her as his daughter.

Who is Janak? Janak is the greatest enlightened king before Rama. Ashtavakra Gita, the highest of the scriptures, speaks of him. Before Janak, it's not even believed that an enlightened king is possible, a fully enlightened king. This is Janak. And Sita is Janak's daughter. She grew up with the guidance and light of Janak.

And Sita, with an enlightened father and later an avatar—a manifestation of divine—as husband, Sita is truly a blessed one. And even more blessed is Janak who has a daughter like Sita.

If you ask Janak, "what is the source of all your inspiration, all your meaning, all your joy?", he would say, "Sita". Rama is a king, but know Rama as a man. He is madly, truly, deeply in love with Sita. And Sita is the **pinnacle of devotion**, of giving herself fully to her man. This powerful phenomenon is Sita.

In the modern mind, we completely take this away from the woman. The archetype of Durga, the independent, powerful, and strong woman who takes the lead, who protects, who nurtures, who knows, who has the eyes to see clearly, who protects, who guards, who advances and who leads by action, this archetype is acknowledged. But in the modern times, **injustice is happening to the archetype of Sita**, the goddess Sita. She is seen as weak, as someone totally devoted to her man with no place for herself. But if you ask Sita, she is complete. She is complete in love. Her life is complete in meaning, her life is complete in fulfillment, her life is complete in oneness. And if you ask Rama, Sita is the inspiration. He can be away from his kingdom for 14 years. People say Rama left his kingdom, but when Sita is with Rama, Rama can be anywhere, wherever Sita is, anywhere. And Ravana dared to take Sita away from Rama, and he saw what came. This is the power of Sita. In her feelings, in her presence, she invokes the highest courage in a man, the highest values in a man. We all know that Rama is a man of values, a man of courage, a man of clarity.

The man, the divine. What is the roots of the divine? It is the love of Sita, the devotion of Sita, the surrender of Sita. An **unbreakable trust**. And when you have such an unbreakable trust, such will, such courage to be so vulnerable in trust, divine manifests in your presence.

Before meeting Sita, before adopting Sita, Janak was a king. After adopting Sita, Janak is an enlightened king. Before Sita came to the life of Rama, Rama was a prince. But after Sita came to life of Rama, Rama is the eternal king. This is the power of woman. This is the feminine power.

But if you tell Sita that "this is due to you. You are at the heart of Rama's success", Sita would say, "no, this is my Rama". Because Rama is her, she is not there. She is Rama.

There is no I, there is no me
There is only love, only trust
Only devotion, only dedication

And such deep trust, such deep perseverance. No matter what is the situation, no matter how is the situation, Sita is **centered in her trust, in her love**. And such patience, in the middle of the difficulties.

In the story, the great epic Ramayana, Sita is taken

thousands of miles away from the forest where she lived with Rama to a unknown land. At that moment, her man is no king. Her man is in the forest, and he has no army, and she trusts that he will come. It is because of her trust that Rama came.

Gravitation, just the very Earth's presence, keeps the whole humanity, the whole life on it, nurturing it. What does it do? The Earth's presence is giving birth to this life. This unknown mysterious force we do not see. We only see the force of action, the force of doing. This mysterious **feminine force of presence**, this is Sita. In her presence, Sita is the call of the divine.

Sita is **wisdom**, she is insight. In the toughest times, she is wisdom. Rama can always resort to her, Rama can always speak to her. The virtues and the values which Rama is so deeply rooted in, the inspiration is Sita.

And the most powerful aspect of Sita is her **purity in love**. She is so pure that no doubt can reach her. No doubt of any kind, no self-doubt, no doubt in her love, no doubt in her man, no doubt reaches her. This is the purity of Sita. This is the powerful purity. Today the world is full of doubt. Self-doubt, doubting the other, doubting love, doubting this, doubting that. In the very innocence of love, Sita blossoms. And when

Sita blossoms, Rama arrives. If even for a moment Sita blossoms in you, Rama arrives. Because Rama is called, that strength, that vision, that power, is called by that inner purity, that inner innocence, that love, the devotion, the surrender, the patience.

And so, it is Sita-Rama. You cannot separate Sita and Rama. If Sita is there, Rama is there. If Rama is there, Sita is there. They are one. Many stories which came after Ramayana tried to separate them, tried to create stories about them. In the original context, there is nothing like that, they are one. They would always be one. Sita-Rama. After 8000 years, Sita-Rama, Sita-Rama.

Jai Sita-Rama
Jai Sita-Rama
Jai Sita-Rama
Jai Sita-Rama
Jai Sita-Rama
Jai Siya-Rama
Jai Siya-Rama
Jai Siya-Rama

That immense commitment, that immense devotion, the deepest, truest loyalty, that nothing remains, only Rama, only Rama. That devotion.

The mind likes to create the idea that, "yes, if Rama is there, I would be devoted". If the "I" is there, you cannot be devoted. When "I" is not there, Rama is there. If it doesn't manifest in your life from outside, the divine would come from within. It would come from the deepest core of your heart. And if you're fortunate, if you have strength of the karmic imprints from the past, then Rama will manifest from outside. But let Sita manifest in you. The purity, the innocence, the love, the devotion, the commitment, the surrender, the loyalty.

Such **loyalty**. Loyalty is often associated with Christian ideas, but there is a deeper loyalty, the loyalty of the soul, the loyalty of trust, the loyalty of surrender, the loyalty of actions.

And this **strength** to follow Rama in the most difficult. He didn't ask her to come. She could have stayed in the palace, all taken care of. She could have gone back to her father. But Sita says, "no matter where you are, I am with you. No matter how you are, I am with you. No matter if we are together or not, I am with you".

No matter how much Ravana tried, Sita is Rama's and Rama's. Nothing whatsoever can move Sita. This is the **will**. This is the will with which Ramayana takes birth. This is the will of the woman. And when the will of the woman arises, it unites all men who stand with values, with virtue. This will of Sita is the power of Rama. This power united everyone, brought everyone together. No matter how difficult are the times, no matter how difficult is the challenge, no matter who you are facing, nothing can stand in the way of this will. The root of this will is in the surrender, in the devotion, in the tenderness, in the purity, in the love of Sita.

Jai Sita Ram
Jai Sita Ram
Sita-Rama Sita-Rama
Sita-Rama Sita-Rama
Jai Sita-Rama
Jai Sita-Rama
Jai Sita-Rama
Jai Sita-Rama
Sita-Rama Sita-Rama
Jai Sita-Rama Jai Sita-Rama
Jai Sita-Rama Jai Jai Sita-Rama
Jai Jai Sita-Rama
Jai Jai Sita-Rama
Jai Jai Jai Sita-Rama

Radha

Om Namo Bhagavate Vāsudevāya

I would like to speak to you from the deepest core of my heart, of the greatest, the most amazing manifestation of the divine feminine, beloved Radha.

Radhe, Radhe, Radhe
Radhe, Radhe, Radhe

Radha, Radha the divine. Who is Radha?
Imagine her with eyes like monsoon skies
Brimming with boundless love for Krishna
Infinite love for Krishna, infinite devotion for Krishna
Her love knows no conditions, no boundaries
It is so vast, the soul doesn't justify it
It's the vastness in itself, the very cosmos in itself
It's deep as ocean

Radha's love is guidance to the power of unconditional, infinite love. Love that doesn't ask, doesn't demand, only gives endlessly, selflessly. Through this love, find courage to open your heart, find the ability to love without fear, without judgment, to let love be your guiding light.

For Radha, love is not just a feeling, it's her very existence
Every breath she takes is a symphony,
a music of devotion
Every beat of her heart is a dance of devotion, of
divine love

And it is **a journey of transformation**. Through this journey of transformation, she expresses her love to Krishna. Her transformation is the expression of the deepest devotion to Krishna. Transformation is bound to happen. Transcendence is bound to happen. Her transcendence is the gift by Krishna, a gift to Krishna. In that surrender, that blessing will take place.

This bhakti is a beacon for all seekers, showing what surrender is.

Radha is an **eternal inspiration**. When Krishna sees Radha, when Krishna imagines Radha, when Krishna thinks about Radha, his flute starts to sing. When he plays for Radha, all the songs start to blossom. It is Radha that is the inspiration. She is the inspiration. And from that inspiration, the expression finds its melody.

Radha is the **true expression of leadership**, showing what it means to lead through heart.

When you lead through love
When you lead through heart
When you lead through devotion
There is joy, there is celebration
There is abundance, there is prosperity
There is health, wealth, vitality

Leading through heart doesn't mean leading through weakness. Heart is the bravest, strongest. It is leading with strength. It is the only true strength. In that strength, in the strength of love, the beauty blossoms, creativity blossoms, art blossoms.

Let Radha in you shine
Rise and shine
Let Radha in you blossom

Radha, the divine manifestation of beauty, of love, of devotion, of inspiration, of leading through heart, leading through love, leading through inspiring, leading through beauty.

When this divine manifestation takes place, beauty blossoms, beauty shines. Beauty is the dimension which brings the divine to this planet, which brings the divine to reality, to manifestation. It's Radha who brings Krishna to this world. It's the love of Radha, the call of Radha, whose longing is calling Krishna to manifest.

For the divine, there is no longing
The divine is in a state of eternal bliss
The divine is in a state of eternal isness
The divine is in a state of isness
Which is infinite and eternal

It is **the longing of Radha** that brings the divine, eternal, infinite alive in the senses, alive in the body, alive in the life. And that call, that longing, inspires divine to manifest, to reincarnate, to come back.

This is the beauty, this is the power of the divine feminine. The power of love, the power of devotion, the power of beauty, the power of inspiration, the power of heart, the power of expression, where love reaches Ananda, where Prem becomes Ananda. Ananda is the place where there is no sense of I, of me, of you, it disappears and only Ananda remains, only the bliss remains. That, that is Radha.

She surrenders in her devotion
She melts, she becomes one
In that state of isness
In that state of oneness
In that state of surrender
Isness and surrender become one.

That is where Radha is.

Radha is the peak of devotion
Radha is the peak of love
Radha is the longing to meet the divine
Radha is the longing to know Krishna
Radha is the longing to meet Krishna
To become one with Krishna

At the call of Radha, the divine manifests. The divine has inspiration, the divine has that inner space. Like when the Earth calls the clouds, the same inner space is created in which the divine manifests, in which Krishna manifests, in which Krishna comes. Now, this state of being, this state of isness, this state of love, this state of divine love, this state of devotion is Radha.

When this devotion, this surrender, this love starts blossoming in your life, you will see the **blessing of Radha**. It's only by Radha's blessing the divine manifests. It's only by Radha's blessing, the devotion manifests.

When you surrender your I
When you surrender your me, my
When you surrender at the feet of Krishna
The devotion blossoms
And in the devotion
Beauty blossoms

Satyam Shivam Sundaram is the highest, and of those, Sundaram, beauty is the highest. After beauty, Krishna comes. **Beauty calls Krishna**. Beauty is deeply rooted in devotion. Beauty which is deeply rooted in the surrender. In this serving, in this surrender, there is no I. And when there is no I, the devotion blossoms. And that surrender can only take place in love. So, the call of love is the call of Radha.

When love knocks on your door, when the flute of love calls you, listen with your heart. Listen with the deepest core of the **flower of love within**. This flower of love might be in a seed state in you, might be in the state where it is in a hard shell. But in that hard shell, there is this tiny spark of life which can turn the whole Earth into a spring. That tiny spark of life, pay attention to that. Don't focus on the shell. That tiny spark of life has so much power, it will break the shell. It will break even the toughest of shells.

Pay attention to this flower of love
See it as fire of longing, as fire of love
Bring your attention through gratitude
Be grateful that you have this
From this, the giant tree of love will rise
The vast spring will blossom

So start. Don't wait, don't postpone. Start now, start from that tiny spark. Believe in yourself. **Believe in that tiny spark of love**. From there, the shell will open. No shell can stand in front of that, no matter how strong, how tough, how old it is, how many lifetimes you have built that shell of wounds, of hurts, of pain. So what?

That tiny spark of life, **that tender space in you is eternal**. No time can stand in front of eternal. No time, no space, no matter how vast and how big it is, can stand in front of infinite, the divine infinite. No matter how vast the space is, the space of whatever you have gathered in your life, the space of "me" and "my" you have built around yourself, it cannot stand in front of that infinite, divine infinite.

No matter how old your story is, no matter which story you are telling yourself, how deeply you have analyzed it, how much you're cherishing it and holding on to it—because without this story, who would you be?—no story can stand in front of the divine. **When the divine comes, all your stories will break**, all your stories will be shattered. That is divine, that is love.

No matter what you tell yourself, when love knocks on your door, you will only hear the song of love, the love song. You will only hear the music of love. And that's the call of love. No matter where you are in life, always open that door. Because that door is your shell.

Deep within, the life is blossoming
Deep within, love is finding its roots
Deep within, the fire of divine love is rising

And when this life rises, when this fire rises, when this fire blossoms, the furthest of the stars feel it. When the love blossoms, the furthest of the stars and the furthest space of the universe feel the fragrance of love.

You might be a sapling right now
Fighting the thunders of life
But remember
You are life, you are alive

You are the dream of the existence
You are the dream of the whole divine infinite
Divine infinite is dreaming through you
Is living and blossoming through you
You are the dream of the infinite

Through your eyes, infinite is alive
And sees, feels, knows, connects
In love, in surrender, in devotion, you become
The messenger, the flute, the music, the song
The fragrance of the divine infinite

So **invoke Radha inside**, and Krishna will come. Become the flute, and Krishna will come. Krishna loves flute. Krishna cannot live without flute. Krishna will come.

Become the flute—hollow, empty
Nothing of I, nothing of me
Your song is my song
Your music is my music
That is Radha

Radhe Radhe Radhe Radhe
O Radhe O Radhe Radhe Radhe
O Radhe O Radhe Radhe O Radhe
Radhe Radhe Radhe Radhe Govinda
Om Namo Bhagavate Vasudevaya
Om Namo Bhagavate Vasudevaya
Om Namo Bhagavate Vasudevaya
Radhe Radhe

Ma Durga

Ma Durga, the embodiment of strength, power, and independence. Shield and sword. Courage, action, strength, authority, and a dynamic expression of truth, of beauty, of devotion.

Ma Durga is the pinnacle of **clarity in action**, decisive action. A strength that is deeply rooted in devotion to truth, devotion to divine, devotion to right action.

Rising from the ashes, continuing when the times are difficult and hard, and there is no hope left in life. She is the **beacon of strength**, of resilience, of empowerment. She is the divine energy that resides within the deepest part of our being and expresses itself in form of strength and power, defying the darkness of ignorance and fear.

She is a symbol of **fearlessness**, and she embodies **courage**.

She **confronts and conquers the forces of evil** and adversity that stand in our way, the challenges that stand in our way. With multiple weapons in her hands, she battles the demons of doubt, fear, and despair, reminding us continuously to fight against the demons of ego, of arrogance, of doubt, of self doubt.

She gives hope when there is none left
She gives light when darkness prevails
She gives justice when injustice prevails

With her mighty strength, she rises in her **spirit of rebellion,** of revolution, standing firm in her clarity. She breaks the chains and pursues freedom, pursues liberty.

She **guards and protects** Saraswati, Mahalakshmi. She protects and guards the knowledge, the beauty, the culture, the art, the innovation. With her sword and shield, she protects abundance, freedom, love, beauty, and truth. She becomes one with the beauty and the truth, she becomes one with abundance in order to protect, in order to guard, in order to give that space, that inner and outer space in which abundance flowers, in which beauty flowers, in which knowledge flowers, in which nurture flowers, in which nature flowers, in which light shines through darkness.

She is the **pillar of integrity,** and her actions are guided by deep rooted values. She stands firm in her convictions, and she guides us to our inner strength, inspires us to overcome any adversity.

She motivates us to face the fears, and she blesses us so we emerge victorious. **The goddess of victory.** She invokes the spirit which guides us to navigate the complexities of our inner and outer lives.

She inspires **courage to face the unknown**, courage to explore, courage to venture, courage to face challenges, to grasp opportunities.

She stands firm and pushes us to **choose the right over easy**, choose the difficult over the comfortable.

Her **compassion** heals us. She holds us like a mother protecting her children.

Her unwavering commitment is to Sathyam Shivam Sundaram, to the truth, to the Shiv, to the consciousness, and to the beauty, to Sat Chit Anand, to the truth, to the divine consciousness and to the peak of love, Anand.

Such is her beauty
Such is her strength
Such are her blessings

Whenever you face challenges in your life, when you invoke courage in yourself in the face of challenges, when you invoke will to continue in the face of adversity, you are offering a divine prayer to Ma Durga.

When evil is advancing, and you stand firm and say "no", when you say "no" to difficulties by facing them, when you say "no" to poverty, when you say "no" to ill health, when you say "no" to injustice, you offer your prayer to Ma Durga.

When you make your place in the world for the divine, when you advance, when you gather courage to face the unknown, you are offering your devotion to Ma Durga.

When you hold power firmly in order to advance beauty, love, consciousness, and truth, you receive the blessings of Ma Durga.

When you choose strength over weakness, when you choose courage over fear, when you choose compassion over hatred, when you choose right action over inaction, when you choose to stand upright and look straight into the eyes of difficulties, of adversities, when you face adversities with courage, when times are difficult, and you gather courage, will, and determination to stay true on your path, stay committed, stay dedicated, you invoke Ma Durga.

When you understand the power of right action, of right organization, when you build strength in yourself, when you invoke strength and inspiration in your people, in your team, when you build a strong team, when you protect and take care of your people, Ma Durga's blessing reaches you.

Durga is independent. She is the **epitome of independence**. With firm and deep roots, she stands tall and kisses the sky. Brave and determined, she demands and commands.

Durga doesn't shy away from using the strength and power of her razor **sharp intellect** and the flow of her clear and **direct communication**.

She believes in wealth, in strength, in power
She advances, she protects, she nurtures

When times are difficult, she inspires
When there is no hope left, she creates
She innovates, she finds ways
Like a river finds ways to the ocean

Try telling a river that there is no way to the ocean, that there are mountains, there are deserts, there are fields. How would you reach? It's the strength of Durga. She says:

I will cut through the mountains
I will make my way through the desert
I will enrich the plains with fertility and vitality
And I will find my way to the ocean

Ma Durga

She is the cloud filled with rain
Reaching the furthest corners of the Earth
To give water to the thirsty

When the evil is advancing, she stands firm like a fortress in order to protect the vulnerable. A sage devoted to consciousness, an artist devoted to beauty, an entrepreneur devoted to creating wealth, Ma Durga is their protector. She is the protector of the mother nurture of nature.

She is firm in her actions, she is firm in her decisions

She knows the value of yes because she has strength to say no
She knows the value of devotion because she has strength for dedication
She knows the value of peace and beauty because she has seen battle and ugliness
She knows the value of firmness because she is tender at heart
She knows fire because she has quenched the thirst of the thirsty
She knows justice because she has seen injustice
She knows strength because she has seen weakness of values

She is the light, she is the action, she is the decision
She is the independence, she is the freedom

She breaks chains, she guards, she protects, she advances

May Ma Durga's blessings reach all dimensions of your life
May the formidable force of Ma Durga protect and guard you
May you invoke the spirit of Ma Durga by becoming that force

Don't shy away from showcasing your strength and your power. Don't shy away from this when you face adversity, because the evil is not shying away from it. Don't shy away from asserting your spiritual vigour, your values.

Seek wisdom, seek compassion.

We imagine Ma Durga as fearsome in her independence, in her strength, but remember, she is the **mother of this universe**. She nurtures, she protects, she takes care. Her fierce love is for her children. She holds her children in her arms.

She is totally, immensely, fully **dedicated to Shiva**, to the consciousness, to the divine. And when this inner strength and nurture find a harmonious balance, Ma

Durga reaches us. When we find a balance of this strength, power, deep nurture, and tenderness inside, Ma Durga's blessings find way to our heart's silence.

When you are going through a difficult time, when you see no hope, **pray to Ma Durga**. How would you pray? By invoking your inner strength, by invoking your determination, by invoking your will, by invoking your courage. When you invoke courage in the face of adversity, when you invoke will when the times are difficult, when you invoke courage when fear surrounds you, when you stand firm when everybody else is breaking—Ma Durga finds a way to your heart, to your life and leads you to victory and eventually to absolute victory. So, invoke the archetype of Ma Durga.

Seek **multi-dimensional growth** in your life, in all different aspects of life.

If you see, Ma Durga is immensely capable of fierceness, of saying "no", and yet she's deeply rooted in profound **tenderness**, in the beauty. The most tender, the most gentle, the most nurturing. Such heartfulness. She's so tender, she's so gentle, she's so loving, so caring, so nurturing, hence she knows the value of independence, hence she knows the value of courage, hence she knows the value of strength, hence she knows the power of standing firm in adversity. So, invoke Ma Durga by encompassing wide expressions of strength, of leadership, of protection, of compassion, of nurture, of beauty, of tenderness, of love.

She's symbol of various **complex structures** like classical music with many different instruments, like a well functioning organization, well functioning order, well functioning systems. When you see everything running smoothly in an organisation, it's Ma Durga's blessing. When you see everything functioning smoothly in a city, in the right order, in the right way, with the meaning of beauty and not just for the sake of it, but in order to serve the divine, Sat Chit Anand, Ma Durga's manifestation would be in that place, in that organization, in that town.

Ma Durga, goddess of independence, the
goddess of boundaries
Ma Durga, goddess of system, structure, order,
and justice
Ma Durga, goddess of advancing, of success,
of competition
Ma Durga, goddess of tenderness, of deep compassion,
of care

Ma Durga, goddess of economic and financial freedom, of freedom
Ma Durga, goddess of authority, of power and strength

May you invoke Ma Durga in your heart and embrace strength, embrace goodness, nurture your family, your community, your people. With this, profound compassion and integrity blessed with abundance and serenity will flower in your life.

Invoking Ma Durga

Ma Durga, the power of strength, the power of human will, the power to stand up for yourself.

To invoke Ma Durga's blessing in your life, understand the power of no, understand the strength of will, understand the power of independence, the power of freedom. When we know the power of freedom, when we know the strength of independence, when we pursue independence, when we pursue freedom on all different levels, financial freedom, freedom of psychological freedom, freedom to think, freedom to say, freedom to express—Ma Durga.

To invoke such strength inside, **pay attention to the inner "no"**, the inner boundaries. If you are living in poverty, I am sure there is this inner "no" coming in you, wanting to say "no" to living a life of poverty. When you give attention to that, you invoke Ma Durga inside. Facing the injustice, standing up for yourself, and fighting is next, but first comes paying attention to the inner no.

Ma Durga is the goddess of independence, the goddess of authority, of power. Durga is the fortress. Build such a fortress in your life, in which tenderness, love, and beauty can flower. Create the strength of success, of authority, of good systems and structures, good order in your life.

Pay attention to all that is limiting you, to where you feel limited.

And with your inner strength, when there is no hope, **find hope**. When you walk the path of hope, when you are able to say no, then you can say yes. If your no know is not strong, the yes will not be strong either, so have the strength of no inside.

How to invoke this strength in your daily life? The way one invokes Malakshmi with gratitude, the way one invokes Masaraswati with curiosity, the way to invoke Ma Durga is through the no. Know the power of no, so you know the power of yes.

Write down 5-10 things you want to change in your life. If you're living in poverty, you would want to fight it, defeat it. If you're facing ill health, you would want to defeat it. If you're facing injustice, you would want to come out of it. You would want to be able to overcome the adversities in your life. If you're facing challenges, obstructions, you will have to fight. And not only outer challenges, but inner challenges also, lethargy, procrastination, weakness of will and values, fear, anxiety, sadness, depression, loneliness, and isolation. Wherever you find these demons, Ma Durga gives you strength to fight them.

The way you identify the things which gives you joy and fills you with gratitude, the strength of Ma Durga lies in **saying no to what limits you**, what holds you, your chains. Bring awareness and attention to that.

And with that, bring awareness and attention to **the power of no inside**.

The no has been trodden down century after century. Look at it, know it. It will not be an easy journey, but with the blessing of Ma Durga, you can cross any difficulty, any adversity.

Ma Durga is goddess of values, so **know your values** and have them in place. Build values, stand for what is right, aim for excellence and fight for it. Reflect on the values of your life, and write down your values. Have clarity of the values in your life. The way Ma Saraswati is goddess of meaning and Ma Lakshmi is goddess of joy, Ma Durga is goddess of values. Value independence, value freedom.

Make good systems, good order, and good structure in your life. With this, Ma Durga's blessing is bound to reach you. Ma Durga is goddess of structure, systems, order. She invokes this, and worshippers of Ma Durga know that it is not solely by aiming and making goals you will reach success but by building good systems and good structures.

If you want good health, then make a good structure for it. Instead of focusing on the aim, on the goal, focus on creating a good structure for it to take place. Having good food around you, having a routine of exercise integrated in your day, and showing up day after day for your yoga class or whatever physical activity you have decided to take on.

If you are preparing for an exam, enrol yourself in the right courses and study. Make yourself a good place for studying in your house. Find education, surround yourself with good books, delete social media from your phone, have those things which gives you education, learning, and show up day after day, day after day. Build a structure, a system which makes you reach. Focus on the systematic approach, the structural approach, focus on order.

Durga embodies the essence of order and justice. Law itself is a manifestation of this divine order. To honour Durga, embrace the qualities of **administration** in your life. Maintain excellent administration in all you do. Develop a clear plan, a well-thought-out strategy, and a robust system to guide your actions. Let your life reflect the order and discipline that Durga inspires. By implementing these practices, you invoke Durga's strength and wisdom, creating a life governed by her divine qualities of order and balance.

What Ma Durga loves is **good order**, so organise your surroundings. Put your workspace in order, put your day in order. Make good systems around you. She's goddess of human supportive technology and systems, so have good technology and good systems in place. Give order to the inner, putting your thoughts in order by writing, by making a structure in your mind.

Ma Durga is goddess of habits, so **create good habits** in your life. If you want to eat healthy, keep healthy food around you. And when you eat healthy, when you keep the discipline of eating healthy, reward yourself. Reward yourself when you keep the discipline of a habit. It can be a small reward, but do reward yourself. With a good system of habits in place, Ma Durga's blessing will reach you.

And show up day after day after day after day after day after day. Showing up day after day is the arena of Ma saraswati, but gathering **the will to show up** is Ma Durga. Saying "no" to the demon of lethargy, procrastination, saying no to having 20 cups of chai in a day, or saying no to the fast food you usually order online.

On the bigger scale, Ma Durga is the goddess of **independence**. Start creating independence in your life. Financial independence, psychological independence. Read great literature, read philosophers, read scriptures to build this inner independence, the ability to think for yourself. As Ma Durga, the goddess of strength, blesses you, you will find strength blossoming within. With this strength comes independence and the profound freedom that it brings. Embrace her power, and let the freedom of self-reliance and inner fortitude illuminate your life.

Build a good fortress of wealth, of authority, of power around you, and guard it and protect this fortress. It is easy to see Ma Durga as goddess of fortress, but she is also the goddess of all that is tender, of the most vulnerable, the most tender aspects of life. Love, beauty, tenderness of heart. So, fortress not just for the sake of fortress, then it becomes a prison, but fortress for the sake of beauty, for the tenderness, for the love, for that which gives you meaning.

She is **protector of all the goddesses**. She is protector of Mahalakshmi, of Saraswati, of Ma Parashakti. So protect the values of Mahasaraswati, protect the values of Mahalakshmi, protect the values of Ma Parashakti, the vitality, the life energy. Build your fortress for that, otherwise it becomes power and strength protecting ego, power and strength protecting one who is not taking responsibility for life and doesn't have any deeper meaning and values.

Power and strength should be protecting the freedom for beauty of art, the beauty of curiosity, the beauty of abundance, the beauty of vitality of life, **protecting the softer values of life**. You can build great nations, you can build great economies, but if the softer values of economy, of prosperity, of economic freedom, of good life are not there? You can build a powerful and strong system, but if the values of art, of culture are not there?

And **leave freedom** for Mahasaraswati, Mahalakshmi. Don't enter in their territory. When one has power and strength, the ego tends to make one move into the territory of Mahasaraswati, Mahalakshmi, Ma Adi Shakti. Don't do that. Ma Durga never enters the territory of her sisters. She protects, she draws up the bridge to the fortress, but entering the territory of her sisters goes against her value of independence.

With strength, with power, with independence, the "I" also arrives, the demon of "I, me, my", the ego arrives. And as we know from the story of Ma Durga, that is the greatest demon she fought. So be aware when you are growing the values of Ma Durga inside, when you are invoking Ma Durga, that you don't in middle go along with the demon. **Fight the demon of ego** and devote the strength, the independence, and the freedom to the softer values of life—to love, compassion, art, creativity, and beauty. Bring the strength and protection to Saraswati, to Mahalakshmi, to Ma Adi Shakti, so they can blossom and flower.

And **never lose hope** in the toughest times, in the toughest adversity, in the toughest difficulties. Invoke Ma Durga. She is with you always and always.

Mahakali

The energy of Mahakali—powerful like a sword
No compromises, zero compromises
A total transformation, a total transcendence
And nothing less than that
Nothing less than complete transformation
Nothing less than total transcendence
This is the force of Mahakali

The force of urgency
The force of vitality
The force of change
The force of awakening

She resides within us in the form of awakening of the consciousness, of Kundalini, the divine energies in the serpent form. Ready to be awakened. Ready to change and transform our life once and for all.

There is no room for compromise
There is no room for "ifs" and "buts"
There is no room for "maybe"

Total transformation—now
There is no future, there is no past
Now—in this moment, this very moment

avi Varma

In its vitality, in its completeness
This very moment is Mahakali

When death knocks on your door, would you say "maybe", would you say "if", would you say "but", would you say "what if"? You have to transcend. You have to transform. Total transformation of the consciousness. That's Mahakali. She seeks nothing less than that. She asks from you everything. Put everything at the feet of Mahakali. Cut the head of ego in you and devote it to Mahakali. Cut the head of "me, my, I" and devote it to Mahakali.

She's the **vital force of change**. The change with which all transformation occurs. She's the force of evolution. It's Mahakali's blessing that we evolve. From a single cell organism to this complex life form. It is Mahakali's blessing the life seeks. Multi-dimensional growth. Life seeks evolution.

Whenever you see transformation, whenever you see change, whenever you see transcendence, whenever you see urgency, whenever you see no compromise, it's Mahakali.

Change, transform, transcend
Not then, not there—now
This very moment, this very life
This very flesh and bones

She asks everything
Because she gives everything

She's the divine transformation
She's the divine transcendence in you

She's the spirit of inner revolution
Of life, of beauty, of love
She's the spirit of inner revolution
Of consciousness within your soul

The vital life force of awakening
Of enlightenment, evolution, involution

The silent revolution within your heart
As infinite unconditional love

She leaves no room for conditions
She seeks ultimate infinite love
She seeks infinite surrender, infinite devotion
Because she gives infinite
She is the mother of infinity
She's capable of bestowing infinity
She shows you the path to infinite

Total transcendence. She takes the finite. She takes the time, the kali. The one who takes you beyond time. The mother of time. The one who takes you beyond past, present and future.

The mother enlightenment
The mother awakening
Nothing nurtures like enlightenment
Nothing nurtures like awakening

Devotion of Kali is not for the feeble, for the weak. Devotion of Kali seeks total surrender, total devotion, total revolution, total transcendence of the soul. Complete awakening.

No compromises. No ifs, no buts. Absolute truth in its purity. Absolute isness. Infinite isness prevailing in all dimensions of life, prevailing in all dimensions of life and beyond.

Kali is death
Death of your ego
Death of your conditioned self
Death of your limitedness

She is the limitless potential in your soul
—ready to be awakened
She is the limitless potential in your life
—ready to shine
She is limitless, she is limitless

Multi-dimensional expansion flowering in every aspect of your life. Shahasra kamal. **Complete enlightenment**.

Within our being she is **the kundalini**, the life force, the vital life force of life energy, full with life.

At the end of our life, she is waiting in form of the death. The blessings of any other goddess is not certain, but the blessing of Maha Kali is certain, because at the end of our lives, whether we live fully or not, death is certain. That is her love.

Whether you see it, whether you face it, know it, forget it, hide it, hide it behind it, death is certain. Nobody escapes death. Ninety or hundred years is nothing more than a blink of an eye in the face of time, in the face of the goddess of time and timelessness.

Living is the way to devote yourself to Ma Kali. Live fully. Respect life because she dearly respects life. She is goddess of death, yet she is the **life affirmation**, the very vital force in our selves seeking evolution and transcendence.

This is Ma Kali.

Om Ma Kali Namaha

She is the symbol of transformation, of liberation, of

freedom. She embodies the ultimate freedom from ego, from ignorance. She guides us towards liberation, she guides us towards enlightenment. Devote yourself to this powerful energy, this vital energy of total revolution within your being.

When the British ruled India, their only fear was Ma Kali. Whosoever put the symbol of Ma Kali in their house, the British used to go after them. Because Ma Kali demands **total freedom**. The first revolution was started by the revolutionaries who worshipped Ma Kali, because they believed in liberation, in freedom, in the very principle of life and liberty, in pursuing meaning, pursuing joy, pursuing awakening, pursuing enlightenment.

Devote yourself to Ma Kali. Seek total transformation, a total revolution within your being, enlightenment. Nothing less than **complete enlightenment**. Ma Kali guides you to this and tells you that it is your right, that this is who you are, this is your nature. And only complete enlightenment takes you beyond life and death and nurtures you to the deepest core of your being.

Ma Kali's love is unconditional. She is the **raw power of maternal love** without any conditionings. She loves you now and forever. She will make sure to guide you through darkness. She makes sure that you are the light to the world, you are the light to life.

The way enlightenment is wrath to ignorance, the same is Kali. She is the enlightenment. When enlightenment shines in you, no ignorance stays, no doubt. Clarity and purity prevails.

The universe was born with the blessing of Ma Kali. The time, the Big Bang. To serve one and only one purpose—the evolution of life, the revolution of life, the ultimate transformation.

In the beginning, the dream of this universe is one, life. And when Earth found life, nothing is more happy than this universe, celebrating. And Ma Kali is the happiest because she is the time. She is the time, and she is the timeless.

Whenever there is a Buddha
Whenever there is a revolution of compassion
Whenever there is a revolution of consciousness, of love
Whenever there is a revolution of inner freedom, of freedom
Maha Kali is the happiest

Devote yourself, and to devote yourself seek nothing less than **total transformation**.

Live every moment as if it is **the last moment**. Live every moment as if it is the only moment. Live every breath as if it is the last breath, the only breath. Let every moment be complete. Whatever you do, do it as that would be your last opportunity to speak, to do, to act.

And **seek excellence** because in excellence, Ma Kali's blessing will reach you. Make a good cup of coffee, make the best. Whether you are a doctor or an engineer, deliver your best, nothing less because that's what Ma Kali seeks, excellence, because through excellence, there is transformation. Not perfection because she knows that nothing is perfect, but excellence, mastery, intensity, vitality, urgency. These are her qualities. These are the qualities she is dedicated to.

So, when you dedicate yourself to the quality of excellence and mastery, when you seek nothing less than total transformation and transcendence of the consciousness, when love transcends into unconditional love, when unconditional love transcends into divine love and compassion, not only now, but for future generations to come, Mahakali's blessings are bestowed upon you.

When you **live every moment as a gift**, when you live every breath as the last breath, when you celebrate life in its fullness, in its completeness, in its is-ness, Mahakali's blessings reach you.

When you ask yourself the existential questions, "**who am I?**", "what is the nature of reality?" and start on a journey to know thyself, you invoke the blessings of Ma Kali.

When you **take the quantum leap of faith** into the divine and shed your limited self, I, and see the ultimate nature of your consciousness in the form of is-ness, you get drenched in the magnificence of the great goddess Kali.

Am I the body?
Am I the thought?
Am I the language?
Am I the identities and attachments?
Am I the belongings?

When you ask yourself these questions, the ultimate awakening is bestowed upon your life. When you seek your infinite nature, when you say yes to life and allow total transcendence, transformation, Ma Kali's blessings reach you.

Om
Purnamadah purnamidam purnate
purnam udachyate Purnasya
purnamadahe purnamevavashyasyate

When you take infinite out of infinite, it is infinite
When you add infinite to infinite, it is infinite
Whatever you add to infinite, it is infinite
Whatever you take from infinite, it is infinite
Infinite at the beginning, infinite in the end

Time attempts to divide infinite into finite by creating past, present and future, by creating here, now, then and there. With the time, the space, which happens from here to there, now to then, also manifests. But all the time and space, all the space and time is in and from and for and will be dissolving again in the infinite.

Invoking Mahakali

Ma Kali the goddess of Transcendence. Ma Kali the goddess of Transformation.

To invoke Ma Kali in your life keep **remembrance and awareness of life as a gift**. 80 years, 90 years, 100 years, maximum 110 years if we are lucky, then death is bound to come. Death is the only certainty in life. With this awareness, with the awareness that death can come any moment, remembering this awareness, that this day could be the last day, this moment could be the last moment, bringing such awareness, bringing intensity to this moment, urgency to this moment and seeing this moment as a gift, not wasting it in habitual way of living, but watching and being aware that this moment can be the last moment. Bringing attention to awareness, to mindfulness, to consciousness. Kali is **transformation**, transformation of consciousness. So bring this awareness to consciousness, to life, as any moment can be the last. By this, we invoke Ma Kali.

Kali is also Goddess of **totality**, of living every moment as complete, committing to life, to life affirmation, every moment.

Kali is goddess of **meditation**, so integrate meditation in your life. Learn meditation techniques. There are 112 meditation techniques in Vigyan Bhairav Tantra[1], there are a few foundational techniques taught by Buddha, and there are several active meditation techniques by

---

1 See the section "Guidance for Practices" for the 112 techniques from Vigyan Braver Tantra

Osho[2]. Learn and integrate these meditation techniques in your life.

Kali is goddess of **commitment**. Commit yourself to values, to love, to consciousness, full heartedly. When you give yourself full heartedly, you invoke Kali.

When you dedicate yourself full heartedly to life, to consciousness, to love, to meditation, when you see that death can come any moment and will certainly come one day, when you meditate with this awareness, you invoke Kali.

Kali is also goddess of **offering**. When you sacrifice your lethargy, your weakness of values, when you commit yourself full-heartedly with all and everything to purpose, to meaning, to life, you invoke Kali.

Kali is goddess of **dance**. Not dance is a learned art, that's the territory of Saraswati, but dance as wildness. So put on music, your favorite music, dance music, and dance. Dance for hours, with intensity. Move with the music. Let your body shake, let your body dance. And after hours of dance, lie down and let go totally. Total relaxation, just completely let go of everything, as if this

2 See the section "Guidance for Practices" for more on Osho's Active Meditations

is the last moment. Do this every day. Dance and let go. If you cannot find hours, then start with 10 minutes of dance with full intensity, and then let go and rest. Don't actively rest, just let go of the body and lie down, and when you open your eyes, have gratitude for the life.

Kali is goddess of **freedom**. Value freedom for the sake of freedom. Not freedom from, that's Ma Durga, not freedom to, that's Ma Lakshmi, how freedom is Ma Saraswati—just celebrating freedom without any to and from, how and why, just freedom, total absolute freedom.

The way time moves in total freedom
The way space moves in total freedom
Is infinite

Kali is goddess of **time**, so deeply appreciate whatever time you spend with your family, whatever time you have in life. Be deeply grateful for time, value time, respect time. Always show up on time. Don't waste time on binge watching, or on social media. Remember the goddess of time. She has given you time to reach your full potential, to find meaning, to find joy, to give wings to your consciousness, to be in love, to travel and see the world, to learn, to create, to make a meaningful difference in the world and humanity, to have meaningful time with the people you love, the people who love you, for transformation, for transcendence.

Kali is goddess of **enlightenment,** of awakening. Remember, consciousness can reach awakening, full awakening, full enlightenment. When you and infinity become one, when you know the is-ness—is-ness knowing is-ness— when your awareness is aware of is-ness, of such-ness, tathata tathata, timelessness.

Kali is also goddess of **destruction,** but destruction of what? Of misery, of lethargy. She protects the life affirmative, and she destroys that which destroys life.

Kali is goddess of **rebirth.** From the destruction comes rebirth. When you lose something in life, know it's not the end, because time continues creating and moving constantly. To take birth, you have to lose the warmth and coziness of the womb. To go out in the world, you have to lose the comfort of your home. To be successful in life, you need to lose your ifs and buts and fullheartedly go for what you want. So don't be scared of losing. The new birth will come.

Let go. Kali is goddess of let go. Practice let go in life. Let go, let go, let go. In the same way birds learn to fly, let go of that which holds you.

Let go
Give wings to your consciousness
Give wings to your love
Give wings to life
Let go

Kali, goddess of consciousness, of transformation, of transcendence.

Jai Ma Kali
Jai Ma Kali
Jai Ma Kali

Questions to Invoke Your Inner Goddess

By engaging deeply with the questions on the next pages, you can invoke and connect with your inner goddess, tapping into the rich and diverse aspects of your femininity.

Journaling

Document your thoughts and feelings as you answer each question. Explore how each goddess's qualities manifest in your everyday experiences.

Identify Dominant Traits

Having answered the questions, consider which goddess archetype you feel most connected to based on your answers.

Inner Inquiry

Having answered the questions, consider if there are any of the goddesses you feel less connected to? How might you cultivate this archetype in your life?

Ma Parashakti (Parvati)

1. Which practices do you do to increase the life force?

2. How do you allow for celebration of life? What stops you from rejoicing life?

3. What role does nurturing play in your life, and how do you balance it with self-care?

4. Reflect on a time when you provided guidance and support to someone. How did this experience affect you?

5. How do you connect with your senses?

Saraswati

1. What forms of creative expression bring you the most joy and fulfillment? How often do you engage in these activities?

2. How do you nurture your intellectual curiosity, love for learning and self inquiry ?

3. In what ways do you share your knowledge and creativity with others?

4. Reflect on a time when your wisdom guided you through a challenging situation. What did you learn from that experience?

5. How do you create space in your life for quiet reflection and introspection and learning?

Lakshmi

1. How do you define true abundance in your life, beyond material wealth?

2. What practices do you follow to attract and sustain prosperity and vibrant positive energy in your life ?

3. How do you balance material success with joy and spiritual fulfillment?

4. How do you ensure that you keep a focus on visioning, dreaming, and taking necessary action in the direction for your dreams ?

5. When do you feel grateful? What stops you from going into this feeling more?

Durga

1. What inner strengths do you rely on during times of adversity?

2. Which personal boundaries do you have? Are there any boundaries you don't have currently but would like to uphold?

3. Reflect on a time when you had to summon great courage. What motivated you, and what was the outcome?

4. Which great challenges have you overcome in your life? How has it affected you to go through these obstacles?

5. In what ways do you act as a protector or guardian for those you care about?

Kali

1. What practices or rituals do you use to invoke a sense of urgency and presence in your life, ensuring that you live each moment fully?

2. What fears do you face head-on, and what did facing them make you feel? Are there other fears in your life you could benefit from facing in the same way?

3. Reflect on a time when you had to let go of something that was not constructive for you? How did this immediate transformation affect you?

4. In what ways do you seek to transform yourself and

your environment for the better?

5. In what ways do you practice living your life fully and authentically, refusing to compromise on what truly matters to you?

Part Two
QUESTIONS TO THE MASTER

Radical Authenticity

I want to be authentic. I've taken the decision that I want to live authentically. But how do I go on from there?

What is authenticity? How do you see authenticity?

Well, authenticity, is first of all knowing yourself, what you want and don't want, what you like and don't like, both inside and outside yourself, knowing your values, what is important for you. And then sticking to that, saying completely "yes" to that, and saying completely "no" to what is misaligned with that.

At the heart of authenticity is **courage**, being brave, gathering courage to say yes or no with full heart and stand with that. Before even finding out what you like, what you want, or what you do not want, it requires courage to stand with "yes, this is what I want. No, I do not want this."

And a step before that is **honesty with oneself**. If you feel that, no, you do not want that for yourself, for your family, for your path, then you feel "no" and you say "no".

The mind quite often plays tricks. "Yes, but no, maybe", and "no, maybe". This is where the authenticity fails, where the pseudo enters, where the fake enters, and the unsure enters.

It's authentic to be "maybe", but "maybe" requires work, because "maybe" doesn't take you anywhere. **"Maybe" is confusing** to yourself, it is demanding lot of resources, but it's important to stay in that "maybe" till "yes" or "no" comes. It's important to look at it, it's important to see, it's important to know.

And true authenticity requires one to **look inwards**, not only focus on outward wanting, because our outward wanting can be quite influenced by many factors. We would not even know that this is me. Some people think they are very authentic, but their ideas are just like sheep following one after another. And that is where it requires courage, to give time to yourself, to know, to seek that "this is what I want".

And before wanting, it's important to **find out what you do not want**, what you say no to. Because yes can be built on the foundation of no. The founding rock of yes, the temple of yes is built on the foundation rock of no. You cannot build a temple of yes without the foundation rock of no, because yes requires ultimate trust. Yes requires trust and yes to existence, yes to this whole universe, yes to the flow of wisdom in this existence, trusting that flow of existence, saying yes to that flow of existence requires ultimate trust.

In order to reach to this ultimate trust, one needs to **build a foundation of no**. The foundation of no gives a strong structure, a strong anchor, with which you can take care of yourself, with which you can nurture yourself, with which your energies are not drained, with which you can heal yourself, and you are not scattered. It gives you time, energy, and space to gather yourself, to have an inner space, to vision, to dream, to feel, to know, to see.

What is a house? A house is saying no to weather by building walls to the weather, because without that, the weather is continuously interfering. The human development only happened when the human said no to the weather and build houses, build something from where they can reflect, they can think, they can feel, they can connect, they can know, they can see and go deeper. And all the arts discovered from 30-40,000 years ago, it is all discovered in caves.

With the no there is time to say yes. But if that no is not there, the yes will never come, and if yes does come, it's going to be a compromised yes. And if it is a compromised yes, it never gathers energy to come out of the atmosphere of pseudo-ness, of fakeness, of untruthfulness.

Gandhi created a revolution. He called it "**truth force**". He said "the truth has its own force". And he stood with this truth force. He said, "I am going to stay with the truth and stay committed to it".

Today we take freedom for granted around the world, but there were visionaries who had courage to say no to slavery, no to limitations, so they could say yes to freedom.

We can find similar **limitations in ourselves**. We are limited by our ideas, limited by our conditionings, limited by our "what if, but, this, that, then", all the different stories we tell ourselves, our fixed mindset, that "things are not possible", that "the great thing happens only to people with resources or people with education" or "I will not be able to do it due to this and this". It requires courage to authentically stand with saying no to whatever is holding you back, whatever is stopping you on your path, on your journey. And from there, yes, we begin.

You can see this on many different levels, for example on the level of thought. You can ask yourself, "is this a thought which is truly originating from my understanding, from my experience?" And if not, then question it.

One of the finest texts, Bhagavad Gita, is so good because the origin is authentic. Arjuna is not acknowledging a single thing he doesn't not understand, and neither is he denying it. He's just being authentic. He's not saying, "I do not understand", he's saying, "I would like to know this. I would like to know this." He's questioning, "is that possible? How would it be in relation to my experience? Can I, how?" And thereby he is authentic. And because he's authentic he is able to say "yes" fully.

But if he believes before understanding, before seeing, if he walks on the path before really figuring it out for himself, before putting it in the right order in his mind, then he will go only halfway before compromising. And that is much more dangerous and difficult, not only for you, but for people around you as well because then neither you nor others can rely on you.

So, it requires a deep **commitment** to being truthful and authentic to yourself. And giving yourself time and space, which can help you to know and understand how. Take the example of the weather. It requires that time and space. Give yourself time and space for reflection, with pen and paper, writing down your dreams, your meaning, especially your "why".

"Why" is one of the most authentic phenomena. If you

want something, you want to reach somewhere, ask yourself why. Is it your call? Why do you want that? Is it directly related to your nature? Is it directly related to the joy you experience? If you are not going to experience joy and meaning on the path towards what you want, then most likely you will not be able to make it. But joy and meaning doesn't mean that if there is hardship, then you won't have joy and meaning. Joy and meaning can be in hardship, in overcoming difficulties. And quite often you don't get the core of it till you actually do it, till you actually know it. Often you only understand it in the process, while you are on the process.

So, you need to be aware, because to reach authenticity **you will fall many times**, and you need to rise again. So, when you are falling, make sure you are not hurting yourself and others and you're not causing long-term damage, so it closes your doors to walk further, or it limits you in certain ways. Keep that in mind.

So, not failing so massively that all possibilities are finished?

Possibilities are never finished, what finishes is time. **What you lose is time and energy**. It requires humbleness to experience time and energy as limited. Energy is an infinite resource, but the energy of the body is a limited resource. You have a certain time with your body, and this time is your resource, and this energy and your freedom are your resources. So, freedom, energy, and time. Energy is infinite, but in the matter it has its limitations. Freedom is infinite, but in relation to others, in relation to world, in relation to nature, it has its limitations. Be aware of that.

So, the **journey to authenticity is an adventure**.

Another challenge people face on this journey is **lack of assertion.** They are authentic with themselves, but they are not able to put their feelings, their values, their thoughts, and their ideas forward.

This is exactly what was taking place in Bhagavad Gita with Arjuna and Krishna. Krishna told Arjuna, "assert yourself. If the lie is advancing with such surety, such unconscious animal-like stubbornness, then why can you not move with your values and consciousness with determination, with assertion?"

You are unique, everyone is unique
Without your unique flowering
Existence is incomplete

See, all trees are unique, and they are all asserting themselves. One tree is not thinking "that tree is blossoming, I want to blossom also", or "maybe I will come in the way of blossoming of that other tree".

One can also experience **cowardice** coming in the way of authenticity, that I would like to assert, but I'm scared that I would not be liked, or I would not be loved or appreciated, or I would not be accepted, or some other consequences would come. You need to step back and see, what is the price if you do not stand with your values? And the price is much worse because then you do not have the truth force with you, you cannot rely on yourself, and you would have lot of unfinished projects burdening you with stress and anxiety, and you would have a life full of regrets and compromises. And there's nothing worse than dying with regrets.

When people on their death bed are asked about their **regrets**, most of the regrets are about meaning, about values, about not being true to one's body through health, not being true to one's relations through love and understanding, not being true to one's dreams by following what gives joy and passion, not being true to one's community and society by giving. These are the most common regrets people have. All the regrets can be zeroed down to **lack of authenticity**, to not being authentic.

The body has its own authenticity which is health. If you're not standing with the body's demand for health, you know what results that will bring.

Mind demands clarity, and if you're not going to read, if you're not going to be curious and inquire about life, if you're living on borrowed ideas which are not authentic, then what will happen?

The authenticity of heart is love, and if you're constantly judging yourself, limiting yourself with ideas of being good enough—good enough for whom, for what? Then what is bound to happen is the fall of authenticity of heart. Love is authenticity of the heart.

Blossoming of consciousness, flowering of consciousness, is being authentic to your consciousness.

Existence has bestowed upon us this ability to create our own self, to create who we are, and what we like. But if we allow the self to be built by spoon-fed education, by already established paths, by our surroundings, and we don't explore what is true to us, then we cannot go further and see the freedom from the self, the deeper wisdom of life.

> *'The privilege of a lifetime is to become who you truly are'*
>
> —CG Jung

Trust in life

I find it easy to trust in my own actions and my own effort, but I find it difficult to trust in existence, in divine.

In the absence of trust in life and divine, the fear finds its roots deep in the soul and there blossoms as flowers of angst, anxiety, fear and the fruit of fear, fear of life itself, being scared of living, scared of life.

What is trust in life? What is trust in divine? Is there divine? Is life in itself divine? What is trust? Trust in what?

Life has its own intelligence, has its own wisdom, has its own flow. If we leave life to the human mind, it will do to life what it has done to the planet, to the nature. You see, when children are born, they are born with joy in their heart, with a smile on their face, and when most people die in their old age, they are full of bitterness, misery, complaints and problems. So, this is what we do to life. We take it away from its intelligence and impose our own stupidity and idiocy on it. This is what the human mind and ego are capable of. And in that, in the middle of that, we firmly believe that we have answers to life because we have given birth to science and philosophy and technology, industrial and capital systems, and societies and civilizations. So, we must be knowing better than the life's intelligence.

But rarely do we see that the instrument we use to advance our civilization is mind, which is a product of evolution, which is a result of evolution. And what is evolution? Evolution is life, intelligence, wisdom of life flowing. Life has its own intelligence, has its own wisdom. But in our conditioned habits, in our conditioned ideas, we go away from this intelligence and impose our own ideologies and conditionings on life.

What we lose by this is the jewel and the diamond of trust—trust in life. This diamond, this jewel, is what we are born with. And then eventually we lose trust in ourselves, trust in love, trust in beauty. We go far away from trust and divine, and our life becomes a breeding ground of fear, anxiety, worries, complaint, bitterness, misery, and it becomes a big problem to be solved, or a tick box, a spreadsheet.

So, what is trust? How to step back from this habitual way of living in fear and come to trust? First understand that trust is the territory of the brave ones, of the brave hearts, because to trust you need to be vulnerable and let go.

Let go of your fears
Of your insecurities and doubts
Of your ifs and buts and thens

Trust in Life

Stand under the blue sky
Drenched in monsoon rain
Rejoice the openness of heartfulness

To trust, you need wisdom to see the beauty, the intelligence, and **the ever flowing wisdom of life**. You need to look up in sky and see the billions and billions of galaxies and stars. So much life, a universe filled with life. How did it come into existence? How is it flowing? See our planet, see how life is, with birds, clouds, mountains, rivers, the sheer abundance and sheer vastness of life and its wisdom—see all this without seeing yourself separate from it, without seeing yourself outside it. Because when you stand outside it and close yourself into your habits and ideas, into your conditionings, into your thought patterns, into your pretty little imagination you portray for the future or the baggage you carry from the past, you miss the wisdom of life.

Human mind stubbornly carries the idea that it knows how things work. The mind has learned some primary school logic and reasoning, certain ways taught in schools which were designed to fill the work force, and so it gets an impression that it knows how life is, what life is, and it gets very certain about it. See people in their 80s and 90s, they are very certain about what life is. And they are right. They are talking about their life, in that particular place of the world, in that particular situation. And they have gathered a certain form of crystallized intelligence, but not the wisdom of life.

With the wisdom of life comes joy, comes serenity, and deep trust in life.

When a baby bird learns to fly, the mother life kicks and forces the baby bird to open its wings. One can portray the picture of merciless mother life kicking you out of the nest. So is life, it kicks you so that you break your shell and come out of it, but when this happens, we make an even thicker shell. When life hits you, we hide in our conditionings, in our ideas, in our habits, in our fears, in our anxieties, in our worries. When love knocks on our door, we hide in our pillows. When divine calls, we look away in our mobile phones. This is how mind is, this is how thought is, this is how our habits are.

Trust is the territory of the brave ones, of the brave hearts, and it requires deep roots in life, in love, in tenderness and vulnerability, and letting go of the fear, letting go of the anxieties. And believing in oneself, believing in one's dreams, believing in one's love for life, believing in wisdom.

Start with believing or start with acting. Just take actions. Let life kick you and open your wings.

In the temple of life, the fool is wiser than the wise
In the temple of life, the innocent heart
receives the gift
Receives the blessing which life bestows upon all

But it's the tender, it's the vulnerable, it's the open, it's the innocent, it's the pure hearted who is capable of receiving that divine gift called trust. The one who can laugh, the one who can see the wisdom in life's absurdities and life's nature, how it unfolds itself.

Life has an intrinsic nature of unfolding and revealing itself, and it is not standard, it is not 'one fit all'. And that's why it looks scary, because to one person life is unfolding and revealing itself in a completely different way than to the other.

And that's the beauty of life. It not only respects you, but it rejoices you in your uniqueness, it rejoices you in your individual expression, it rejoices you in your magnificence. And it embraces you in your imperfections. It embraces you the way you are, without any if's and but's, this and that.

And if life embraces you for who you are, if mother embraces you for who you are, then it's time for you to embrace yourself for who you are, how you are, because you're perfect. All is perfect because you're divine, life is divine.

Through life, divine unfolds
And divine is perfect
So let life kiss you, let life embrace you
Let life nurture you through its wisdom

But we expect. **We have ideas how life should unfold**. "If this happens, then that should happen, and this should happen", "if this is secure, then I will be there", "this should be like this, so that I can be like that", "all my finances should be secure", "give me an insurance that I will stay healthy". "Give me an insurance that I will face no challenges and it will all be safe". And life answers.

That is not my territory
It is the territory of the death
My land is the waves of the ocean
My land is the flowing river
My land is the stormy nights
My kingdom is the kingdom of life

Trust in Life

Those who trust, those who are brave are welcome
And those who shy away in their fears and habits
In order to reach security and certainty
They have to wait till the death open its door
Because in my kingdom, there is a promise
of life, of love, of beauty, of the adventure life brings
full of experiences, full of wonder,
full of awe, full of magnificence.

O you brave one, come to my kingdom
Kingdom of life, kingdom of love
Kingdom of beauty, kingdom of wonder
Where the nectar of life flows
To the trusting hearts
Where the nectar of life flows
To the brave ones facing the thunder

Let your heart wonder
Let your heart wonder

Let go of all the packages
All the pains, the if's and but's

Open your heart, open your wings
Open your heart, open your wings
Open your heart, open your wings
Open your heart, open your wings

And let life kick you hard so you can fly.

Your consciousness has a potential of the vast infinite sky. Your heart can reach to the depth of oceanic love. And your eyes can be full of wonder and awe, trusting in life, trusting in life, trusting in life, trusting in life, trusting in life.

True happiness

What is the essence of true happiness, and how can it be achieved and sustained?

Happiness, the most sought-after phenomenon in the world. We seek it in our achievements, we seek it in success, we seek it in money, we seek it in love, we seek it in our material possessions, in our travels, experiences, happiness.

If we ask the scientists, they would quickly describe it as brain chemistry. If we try to put happiness in words, quite often it is associated with memories, experiences from the past and wishes for the future. Around the world, it is measured through happiness indexes, and countries compete for being in the top.

So, with different definitions for different people, happiness stays the most sought-after yet most mysterious phenomenon. And technology has made it even more complex—from social media apps to dating apps, from binge watching to food ordered at the click of button, from online shopping to offline shopping. Every month a new gadget, a new technology, a new style, a new fashion arriving in the market.

The most mysterious and most sought after

phenomenon—happiness. How to achieve and sustain happiness?

The longest conducted happiness research at Harvard found that people with meaningful relations, people who take good care of their health and relations and had purposeful work came out on the top of happiness achieved and sustained. But when asked what makes you happy, many people come to wishes and memories.

So, from the perspective of science, philosophy, and psychology, happiness is a complex phenomenon, but from the perspective of life, **happiness is deeply rooted in meaning**.

Meaning differs depending on the situation your are in. Our body finds meaning in health and long life. Our pursuit of happiness in life has one meaning when our needs are fulfilled and another meaning when our needs are not fulfilled. For somebody living in a war zone, where even the basic needs are not met, just meeting the basic needs becomes the whole motivation for life, just surviving. Somebody struggling to make the ends meet, somebody trying to overcome a difficult situation in life, and somebody whose needs are met but who is now facing the deeper questions of life, like "what is the purpose of life?", "what is the meaning of life?", and "what is life?"—at various stages in life, we have a different perspective on happiness, but one thing is constant in all, meaning.

When we **give meaning to the body** through health, it finds happiness.

When we **give meaning to life**—through spending time with people we love, with people we cherish, through celebrating life in a meaningful way, with wonderful experiences and memories, through our work filling our life with purpose, through a mind full of curiosity and wonder, through a heart filled with love—life gets a new meaning. When we work together to a higher purpose, to something greater than our mundane lives, meaning is giving direction to our life.

And when all our needs are met, the bigger questions of life might start to bother us, and life takes us to new dimensions, to new territories, asking, "who am I? What is life? What is the nature of reality? Why are we here?"

This journey, full of wonder and adventure, opens new doors for us. Or it may go in a new direction of having a meaningful life, spending time with family, with people we love. So, happiness is a complex phenomenon, and there is no "one size fits all".

A heart filled with gratitude
A mind filled with curiosity and wonder
The body shaping and crafting health
Meaningful expression of beauty and love
Sharing this journey with loved ones

When facing difficulty and adversities
Standing tall with courage

No matter how difficult is the situation
No matter how high is the mountain
No matter how dark is the valley,
There is always light at the end of the tunnel
Always

The ability to give meaning when there is none
The ability to see light at the end of the tunnel
To gather courage and will when there is none

There is no set recipe for happiness, so **cherish life as a gift**.

Live every moment as a gift
With a heart filled with wonder and curiosity
A spirit of adventure as if it were the first moment
A mind with urgency as if it were the last moment

Celebrate life, and life will find
Joy and meaningful happiness

Meaning can be sustained, happiness cannot. Even the attempt for sustainable happiness is foolish, but a meaningful life is definitely possible. Meaningful relations are definitely possible. And from that joy comes.

Happiness is superficial
Joy is deep like ocean

Pursue meaning, and build a good life for yourself and others through life affirmative principles—freedom, compassion, and joy.

Celebrate life
With a heart full of gratitude
And eyes filled with sparkle
Rejoice! Rejoice! Rejoice!

Joy of life

How can I get out of the tendency to focus on problem solving?

Life, a wonderful gift. The most mysterious, absurd phenomenon. We don't know what's next, how it's going to turn out, what's going to happen.

The more we try to understand it, the further it goes away from us, and the further the understanding of it goes away from us.

The more we try to seek the meaning of life, the more we find the absurdity, the irony, the imperfection, and somctime the meaninglessness of it as a whole. We can give meaning to it, but if we just see it directly, I doubt it has any.

So, this is the funny aspect, the funny life, and **the only sensible approach to life is humour**—seeing the comedy of life, how it unfolds and what it is, and rejoicing the awe of it, the beauty of it, the magnificence of it, and living the mystery of it instead of constantly trying to understand it and solve it, and either make it into a problem to solve or a goal to achieve or something somewhere out there in the future with the baggage of the past. By that we are missing what's here with us in this moment.

Instead of embracing life and hugging it the way it is, we are always looking for imperfections in it, giving our attention to solving it in order to reach somewhere, or getting crushed under the weight of the fear and anxiety, or being bugged by constant complaining about something.

So, this is life, and what we're going to speak about today is joy. Can you point exactly to what joy is? Pay attention and try to see what joy is. Is it one particular phenomenon we can find? Or it is **a complex wisdom that appears** when we see the absurdity of life and embrace it the way it is? When we see the imperfection of life and cherish it and appreciate it the way it is. When we celebrate the gift of life, the gift of this moment alive because we're not sure what's coming next. When we see the wonder of life, how we are alive, what a wonder life is, what a blessing. When we share this blessing with others, when we receive this blessing from others, with openness, tenderness. When we find humor in the absurdity and irony of life, in this complex alchemy—joy appears mysteriously.

A heart filled with joy
Eyes filled with wonder
A spirit of rejoicing

Celebrating, gratitude
A mind fascinated by awe,
Intrigued by humor and irony

—in this, the highest of the wisdom, the joy appears. When we can laugh at our stupidities, at our foolishness, at our seriousness.

When we are making life into a problem, a utility, or a goal to reach, we go far from this wisdom. Too smart for yourself. And in that, one misses the life, one misses the spring, the full moon light, the smile, the wonder in the eyes.

Rejoice and celebrate the innocence in your heart because that's where the spring of joy blossoms. Joy is the highest of the wisdom, the greatest of the insights.

Stay foolish, stay innocent
That's the wisdom of joy
Let your heart be full of gratitude
Your eyes full of wonder

Your misery and your seriousness is ugly.

Choose the beauty
Choose love, choose joy
Choose the wonder and awe
Choose the celebration

You're not a nut and bolt of a big machine, you're a human being destined for the spring of consciousness, destined for love, for life, for celebrating life, for seeing its wonders, for rejoicing in it's beauty.

The laughing Buddha, the celebrating Buddha, the dancing Buddha, these are some of the symbols of joy in the East. The laughing Buddha seeing the humour of life, the dancing Buddha seeing the celebration of life, the rejoicing Buddha seeing the wonder, the awe, and the beauty of life.

Drop your misery. Let go of your ideas and celebrate. Dance your dance, sing your song, and let creativity blossom in your heart.

Take the empty canvas, the colours of life, and let your brush dance—in absence of self doubt, self sabotage, and self criticism. There's no one to judge, there's no one looking. You and life alone.

Celebrate your life because death is certain. Death is certain, and the only way you can beat it is by living every moment, living every moment to the fullest.

Life is now and here
This very moment
This very moment

In the depth of winter I finally learned that within me lay an invincible summer

—Albert Camus - On Joy

Find your invincible summer
Find your invincible summer

'I'm too intelligent, I'm too demanding, I'm too resourceful to simply celebrate life'

—Jean Paul Sartre

'The surest sign of wisdom is cheerfulness'

—Michel de Montaigne

Live dangerously my friend
Live with celebration
Because life is uncertain
Only death is certain

Whatever, whosoever you have in your life, whosoever you are with, celebrate—only death is certain.

Life is absurd, meaningless. Whatever gifts it has bestowed upon you, take it as a blessing and live it. Neither it's a problem to be solved nor is it a utility to be produced.

Joy is a natural state which is there. You would never see a miserable child, all children know joy, but with time, with our education, you have to be useful, you have to reach somewhere, you have to produce, to add value to the money which is already printed 30 years ago, you have to add to the GDP, you have to have a career, find meaning, find happiness,. You have to, have to, have to. In this all 'have to', you drop the diamond of joy which divine sent you, and what you are left with is bag of misery, of ideas, and a cunning and clever mind.

Celebrate oh my dear friend
Rejoice oh my dear friend
Only death is certain
Only death is certain
Only death is certain

Whatever gifts of life bestowed upon you
Embrace it with open arms
Only death is certain
Only death is certain

Laugh at the irony of life
Laugh at the absurdity
Only death is certain
Only death is certain

Live courageously
Live dangerously

Whatever moments of life are given to you, whatever moments of life you have—rejoice, rejoice, rejoice my dear friend.

Only death is certain
Only death is certain

The Power of Presence

What is this moment? What is presence?

These are quite common words used in spiritual settings by people who meditate. There is a famous book, 'Power of Now' by Eckhart Tolle, and many mindfulness teachers and gurus say, "bring your attention to the present", and many of the ancient mystics are talking about presence, being present, feeling your presence, about presence in itself, and about being in the moment. What exactly does this mean?

The mind has a tendency to go either into the future or into the past, or analyzing something from the future or from the past in this moment. This is how the mind moves. It is always going into the future and into the past. Or it is busy doing something, thinking. It is busy.

So, when you bring your attention to the present moment, in the present moment, attention generally comes to body because body is just present in this moment, it is not going into the future. And attention also comes to senses. Senses are also present in this moment. And by this, we free the space of the mind because mind is constantly busy.

Now, in that short period when the attention is free

from past and future and it is in the present, in that moment, in that time, **the moment comes alive**. This very moment comes alive, because generally the tendency of the mind is always doing or being busy or in the past or future. And the experience of this moment is not available to the mind.

So, many meditation techniques are bringing your attention from this constant doing, from this constant busyness to isness, to this moment.

Now, what exactly is this moment? There is no such thing as the moment because time is moving. Time is a movement, it is moving, but when you pay attention, the moment comes alive. So, whenever you are capable of paying attention to the present, that moment is the moment which comes alive. And it's important for the mind to experience awareness in this moment so it knows other than the past, other than the present.

And that is why there is so much attraction to alcohol, to sex and other things that bring people to the moment. People go skiing or sailing in the ocean. These experiences bring people to the moment.

But you can learn to bring yourself to this moment. Then you have the freedom to bring yourself to this moment without being dependent on something outer.

There are people who come to this moment through **physical activity**, like sports, or by action, by doing. When you are busy, and you get into the flow of doing, and you are in a **good flow**, the mind's attention come to the moment. In that moment also, you start to feel the presence, to feel your presence, to feel this moment. Or when your **senses are fully awake** from a good connection with nature, running, after a cold shower, being in love, listening to music, then also the attention comes to this moment.

There are many **meditation techniques** for bringing attention to now, like Vipassana and Zazen, or people go to satsangs and discourses. Most of these techniques are about mastering attention and bringing it to this moment, bringing it to the senses, bringing it to the body, bringing it to the breath. Being aware of mind, of thought, of emotions. Many mindfulness techniques are about this, but at the heart it is mastery of attention and awareness, and through this mastery knowing consciousness.

Consciousness is a mysterious phenomenon. The science has tried to understand it, psychology has tried to understand it, biology has tried to understand it, and they all described it in different ways. "This is a phenomenon of the brain", "this is how it is", "this is a phenomenon of the brain chemicals". Howsoever it is, whatsoever it is, we all would agree that consciousness is the phenomenon which makes us aware of the life.

This consciousness is available to us, and the more conscious we are, the more aware we are, and the more we have mastered directing our attention, the more we can direct our attention to the right places. And bringing attention to the presence gives a better experience of life.

So, this is a good start of meditation. Meditation is not limited to only being present, only being in this moment, it is a much vaster phenomenon, but this is a good start, a good foundation—mastery of attention.

Overcoming Problems in Meditation Practice

I am struggling with sleepiness and falling asleep when I try to meditate.

Firstly, this is natural because in meditation your mind starts to have deep relaxation, and that relaxation is the time when the brain nurtures itself, when the brain finds healing. Our modern day lifestyle is very demanding to the mind, and it is very demanding to the brain. The body gets its nurture during sleep, and some part of the mind and brain also rest, but rebuilding, nurturing, and coming to a point of deep relaxation, this requires much more than sleep, this requires a state of meditation.

If you accept that you are falling asleep and allow sleep to come, and you say "yes, this is natural, this is fine", and you do not judge yourself, you do not resist it, you do not fight it, you allow that, then slowly with time the brain would find that rest it needs. When you are consistent and persistent with meditation, the brain would find that rest, and it would change, you would not be sleepy.

Secondly, what happens in meditation is that relaxation comes, and with that relaxation the awareness diminishes, because relaxation also brings sleepiness, so awareness starts to disappear. If you can invoke awareness through active meditation, through dancing, or through Osho Active Meditations, or through breathing, or through humming, then you can take awareness into relaxation. You would still be relaxed, the brain would still have the same nurture—actually even more— to restructure itself, to reorganize itself and then come back to healing, and from there, you have awareness along in the deep rest.

So, these are two different ways. Do both of them. One is just allowing the sleep to come, that's fine. Just make sure that you are not lying down, that you still stay sitting. Allow it, don't fight it. Find yourself a decently comfortable position, like with a back rest. Find yourself a good chair, and it's okay to fall asleep. Slowly, slowly you will stay awake during meditation practice. The second way is, before entering in meditation, take a cold shower, do active meditation, do pranayama, do something which wakes your body up. These are two methods. Go with both.

During deep meditation, when you are sitting with straight back, like in the Zazen position, and you allow yourself to sleep, the body is sleeping, the brain is regenerating—in that moment a deep silence comes, deep silence. Now there is wakefulness, you are awake and yet sleeping, both at the same time.

In Bhagavad Gita, the yogis stay awake in the sleep. This is what it is. And it is possible, it's completely possible that you can sit with straight back, totally calm and fully in sleep. This is the third way, and all three ways work.

The first way is saying, sleep is okay, let the brain nourish itself through sleep and deep rest. The second way is to wake yourself up through cold shower, through pranayama, through active meditation, dancing or music, and then go to meditation. And the third, Zazen, keep practicing and eventually the sleep will come, and you are awake yet sleeping. The body and the brain are sleeping, and yet you are awake, yet the mind is fully awake. It's like mindfulness at its best. So, that's fine. All is good. So, all three—this is a practical approach for this.

Am I supposed to do all three at the same time?

No, that is a spontaneous choice. It depends on the time of the day, whether you are tired after a long day of work, how you are feeling, what is that moment. The third way requires you to be meditating continuously for a few hours, or a few days, or being in a deep meditative retreat. The second way depends on the time of the day. If it is early morning, then active meditation or taking a cold shower is well suited, and if it is afternoon or evening then Osho Kundalini Meditation because it takes the stress of the day out of the body, or giving the body a flow through dancing, and then entering into the meditation. That also works. And if you are just meditating spontaneously and at that time you're falling asleep, that's perfectly fine. You can fall asleep, that's okay.

Now, on some occasions you do not want to fall asleep because you really, really want to be aware. Then a method or technique you can use is urgency, like "this is the last moment, and this is what's happening in this moment, it's absolutely crucial. This is the moment". In that moment bring urgency—total urgency. That's a path you can take.

So, it is more of playfulness. It is not so serious if you fall asleep. If you fall asleep, don't be hard on yourself. But if you need to bring urgency, then bring urgency full heartedly. What is sleep? You can sleep later. You would have better sleep later because now there is that awakening, that awareness, and nothing nourishes our mind as awareness, as consciousness, a deep restful consciousness, a deep restful mindfulness, deep restful awareness. This is the best nourishment for brain and mind, because mind organizes itself. It finishes whatever emotions remain, whatever tasks remain, whatever it needs to organize. And from that deep restful sleep or deep restfulness, the brain nourishes itself.

The two ways the brain receives the most nourishment is REM sleep which happens around 2 to 4 o'clock in the night where it's complete deep sleep, and in a deep meditative state. These are the only two times the brain nourishes itself. The mind organizes itself through dreams, through sleep and in different ways. The body needs sleep, 6-10 hours, depending on the day and the situation, and the brain needs the deep restfulness that happens in REM sleep and in deep meditation.

If you feel that you need to be fully awake this moment, you don't want to be at the mercy of just falling asleep, then bring **urgency**. See this moment as the absolutely the last moment, and pay full attention. Or see it as the first moment, and bring vital freshness, complete curiosity and awe, as if it's the first time you are seeing your mind, the first time you are sitting in meditation. This is the **beginners mind, the Zen mind**. You know nothing about meditation, and you have just entered into the meditation as a total freedom, completely new. So, urgency and the Zen mind, the beginners mind, these two works.

When I'm sitting in Zazen, I don't really know what to focus on, what to aim for, what to expect, what not to expect.

Very good question. See, firstly there is a big misunderstanding in the world that meditation is for everyone. Meditation is a fairly new phenomenon. Yes, Buddha was a pioneer who introduced people to meditation. Around the time Buddha was introducing meditation, just 40 years before, Mahavira founded the principles of meditation. People know about Buddha, but very few know about Mahavira. Meditation had been in Mahavira's tradition for 10,000 years, but meditation in a simple form for everybody was an innovation introduced by Buddha. Before that, was there meditation? Yes, but it was not called meditation. In Vigyan Bhairav Tantra, Shakti is asking Shiva, "what is the nature?", and Shiva answers with different techniques[1]. He does not call it meditation techniques, because then it becomes like you are doing something, and you have a goal to reach.

1 See the section "Guidance for Practices" for guidance to the techniques.

This is the pitfall many Buddhist monk fall into. They are working on it, and they have a goal to reach, either enlightenment or compassion or mindfulness or awareness. **Goal is the territory of the mind**, goal is a territory of thought. Goal is not a territory of heart, goal is not a territory of life, because life in itself doesn't have goal, life in itself is the goal, love in itself is the goal. So, when life in itself is the goal, when love in itself is the goal, then it is not about like reaching somewhere. That's why previous to Buddha, meditation is not a phenomenon which is identified.

So, Buddha did a lot of good in the world by identifying this phenomenon called meditation and putting a label on it as meditation. But side effects came along with it. Monks dedicated to meditation in order to reach a goal, a good goal. They have a good goal for humanity also, peace and non-violence for the world, and for themselves they have good goals, but it is still a territory of the mind.

When it comes to life, when it comes to love, you are complete. Love is complete, love is total, love in itself is the goal. Life in itself is beautiful. Like a seed is complete, a sapling is complete, a tree reaching flowering is complete, a tree in a full spring of flowers is complete, and a tree heavy with fruits is complete. **Life in itself is complete**.

But if you ask the seed, then yes, it wants to reach flowering, but it is not going to reach flowering by chanting "flower, flower, flower, flower". It will reach flowering when the life inside is blossoming and breaking the shell, and it is coming out.

There is no hard and fast rule for the way to come out of the shell. It doesn't work. You can take a rock and break the seed, like a monkey does. And that's what happens to a lot of monks. They become like a monkey trying to break the seed, asking themselves why life is not coming out, why enlightenment is not coming out of it.

It is about **giving it the right soil**, the right nurture, the right weather. And by this, the sapling comes out. And it needs to fight to come out. It needs to fight the challenges, the battle of life. All the ups and downs of the world, of the mind. It goes through everything.

Buddha himself went through all that. At the age of 29, he left home, but before that he went through a lot. He got a very good deep education of awakening, of watchfulness, of Vedic scriptures. He learned a lot in that education. And then he went out, going through so many paths. He was staying hungry, he was doing yoga, he was working with samanas, he was living as a forest dweller, he was living with the monks, he practiced all different kind of praṇayamas and yogas. It is a totally different journey he is on. He is seeking answers.

And there is no hard and fast rule, that that is your journey. **Your journey is your journey**. Meera's journey was her own journey, she went through that journey, and Sahajo went through her own journey. All the enlightened women, all the awakened women had their own journey. Your journey is unique to you.

So, **celebrate your life the way it is**. The way your journey is, that is the best. There is no other journey suited for you. Your journey is the best, your life is the best, and it is complete. Because this is the way. So, whatever life is around you, that is your path. Celebrate it.

And meditation is not necessarily your path. It can be. If it is coming to you, welcome it, see it. There is no hard and fast rule that meditation is always the path. Meera never meditated, yet she is complete, Radha never meditated, yet she is complete, Sita meditated, yet she is complete. So it all depends. Sita was is living in the forest which is the best place for meditation. What else would you do in the forest if you are not meditating? After all, meditation is the best way to connect with the trees. The Zen monks who live in the forest, when they are meditating, they start to go deeper in the nature. The birds sound clearer through their meditation, they feel the fresh breeze more, the senses are much more aware and sharp in meditation, and the energy is much more vibrant in meditation. So, integrate meditation in your life.

See, there is no specific rule for everybody. Now, the mind would say, "yeah, but then my rule is not meditating". Or someone may think "oh, then meditation is not for me". No, you can only say that by doing it first. Do it, go for it, and let's see. There are 112 techniques of meditation, for now we are calling it meditation techniques, in Vigyan Bhairav Tantra[2]. They are not given as meditation techniques though. So, learn different techniques and integrate them into your life.

So, when you are sitting in Zazen, what is in the process, what to expect and what to do? First understand **what is Zazen**. Zazen is just sitting. Zen comes from the word Jhan, and Jhan comes from the word Dhyan. Dhyan just means paying attention, that is the literal translation. How do you pay attention? Through Vivek or conscious

---

2 See the section "Guidance for Practices" for more on Vigyan Bhairav Tantra

awareness. Wakeful awareness. Now, what do I mean by a wakeful awareness? When you are paying attention with the intention of paying attention, that is Dhyan, that you are making sure you are paying attention—that is your commitment. Now, what does this commitment mean? This commitment means that whenever you are not paying attention, you are aware of that also. Jiddhu Krishnamurti expresses it beautifully, "when you are attentive of inattention, that is meditation". So, when your attention comes to your inattention, that your mind has been drifting, and your attention comes back naturally without you bringing it back, but it comes back by sheer remembrance—that is meditation. These were also the words of Buddha when he left his body, "Samyaksamriti", the right remembrance. Remember. Remember what? Remember awareness, remember paying attention.

Now, the mind says, "pay attention to what?" When you are sitting with your back straight and paying attention, what would you pay attention to?

Pay attention to your body. Your body is there, you are not getting out of the body suddenly, like falling, you are sitting in your body. The body has different sensations, a little sensation here and there. Pay attention to that.

What else is there? Your breath. You are not going to suddenly stop breathing. Breath is there. **Pay attention to the breath**.

What else is there? The mind is there, and mind has thoughts coming and going. If you look closely, mind has imagination, mind has memory, mind has thinking and analyzing, mind has projecting something into the future. Different images, random images, random phenomena, spontaneous images, spontaneous phenomena. So, mind with all its thoughts, all its ideas, thinking, images, memory, projections and all the emotions coming to it. **Pay attention to the mind**.

Now, all of this may invoke some kind of **emotion**. You may remember something, "oh, I needed to finish that", and then a little emotion will come. Maybe the thought will invoke some anxiety, maybe it will invoke curiosity, and some questions will come. Then you may start thinking, and it's okay. Think, just pay attention to the thinking. Don't try to stop thinking, because if you try to stop it, you are in this goal of reaching to peace or something. That's not going to happen. Don't try to stop it. Just pay attention to what is happening.

Then what else is there? Senses. All the senses are there. **Be aware of the senses.** Hearing, you hear a sound, and then the mind will go to that. You will hear. You will feel, like feeling the tough of your hands resting on your legs. Notice that. And when you breathe, you feel the sensations in your nose. Pay attention to that. Be aware of the senses.

In Zazen it's recommended to keep the eyes half open, but you can also keep your eyes open. The best is half open, because it's like a central place. With closed eyes you can fall into dreams, and you can fall into sleep, and with open eyes you can start looking around and thinking. The best is half open eyes. To practice, closed eyes is fine and open eyes is fine, because attention has nothing to do with open, closed or half open eyes. Attention is attention. You can keep your eyes half open, that is the best to start with, but having closed eyes is also fine. Keeping the eyes open is a little more advanced.

Now, tantra says, Matra of the senses—that the senses are there, but there is awareness of the senses. The senses you are aware of, the mind you are aware of, the emotions, which is a big part of the mind, that you are aware of, the body you are aware of, the breath you are aware of, and sensations in the body you are aware of. All this is happening. This is Zazen. This is how Zazen is.

In Vipassana you keep bringing your awareness back to breathing. Vipassana originally means ihipasyako, watch it the way it is. That's also the meaning of Zazen, but Vipassana has been taught as bringing your attention back to breathing, because the mind is in habit of doing something, so if you give it a task; bring your attention back to breathing, bring your attention back to breathing, bring your attention back to breathing, then the mind is not feeling bored, going like "okay, now what?", or it doesn't go to sleep because you are doing a task. But that has its own trouble. You can end in an infinite loop of watching the breath. I know people who are in 10 days Vipassana, 20 days Vipassana, 30 days Vipassana, 40 days, and they think they are advancing somewhere in life. Some of them might be, very few, but many of them may be just in a loop, an infinite loop, like a monkey trying to catch its own tail. So, know that. Vipassana has a place in the beginning, and it has a place when the mind is going here and there, behaving like a monkey mind. Then you can bring your attention back to breathing, but it is not a hard and fast rule. So, this is Zazen.

Now, Zazen doesn't talk about bringing your attention to the seer who is watching, to the observer, to the witness, as they do in Vedanta. **Witnessing the witness,** watching the watcher. This is the original form of meditation, the most ancient form of meditation, but it's is little more complex, a little more advanced. I like Zazen because eventually, after the mind has gone through all the different phenomena, after it has done all its monkey mind stuff, after it has gone through the body, after all this, the mind eventually comes to the observer. This is bound to happen. It will take place because it's a natural phenomenon.

In Zazen they don't even talk about the observer. They never mention the observer, they never mention the witness. They never mention it because they see the witness as an illusion. Buddha calls it '**No Self**', saying that the observer you have been witnessing is an illusion. But this is like telling a fish that there is ocean. How would you describe the ocean to a fish? You cannot describe the ocean to a fish. So, the point is not going into whether the observer is an illusion or not.

The Vedantics don't call the observer an illusion, they see it as **Self**, which is constructed over time through different ideas and ideologies. They say that it is a constructed Self, with ego and all the identity which is formed around the observer, the Self. The Vedantics have a more scientific approach, whereas Zen is much more pragmatic and practical in their approach saying, "yes, it is there, but we cannot say anything about it because you would not understand. What is the true truth for you at this moment is body, mind, thought, emotions, senses, sensations, and breathing, so pay attention to that, and eventually on the journey you will discover it for yourself". So, that is Buddha's message. Later the Buddhist priests started to say that there is No Self, and they started to talk about it, and it became a bit complex for people to understand.

So, at this stage the best is Zazen. Observe breath, body, mind, emotions, senses, sensations, and if it becomes difficult or boring, keep bringing the awareness back to the breath. But don't let it become an infinite loop, like a monkey trying to catch its tail. Then you can end up like some people going from one meditation retreat to another, never able to integrate meditation into their daily life. Or not really paying attention—meditation—the original meaning of Zazen.

Part Three
GUIDANCE FOR PRACTICES

Vigyan Bhairav Tantra

Vigyan Bhairav Tantra, one of the finest and most beautiful texts, a dialogue between Shiva and Shakti—Shakti, the divine manifestation of life and all its energies, Shiva, the pinnacle of consciousness, the highest of the high. Shakti is sitting in the lap of Shiva, asking, Oh Shiva, what is your reality? What is this wonder-filled universe? What is this life beyond form pervading forms? And Shiva answers with 112 meditation techniques. Awareness, attention, feeling, rejoicing, celebration, embracing this vast infinite life in oneself through this wonderful present from Shiva to Shakti of meditation techniques.

Most of the meditation techniques in the world have their origin in this conversation, in this dialogue. Whether it is visualization techniques, awareness techniques, centering techniques, feeling techniques, practices, all of the foundation of all the techniques goes back to this wonderful scripture of Shiva and Shakti. Here are the first seven of the techniques:

Awareness of the breath

The first technique is awareness of the breath. Shiva says, when the ingoing breath and the outgoing breath fuse, meet, at that instant, see and feel and know and touch that center, that point which is filled with energy yet is beyond, which is like Shiva Linga, fully surrounded by energy and yet the divine infinite at the center of it, beyond energy. Finding this place where the inhale and exhale meet, when the breath turns, when the outgoing breath is turning to inward flow, when exhale is turning to inhale, when inhale is turning to exhale, bring your attention to this point and let awareness and attention center there. This place is your door to Shiva and Shakti.

At the heart of this technique is awareness, is attention. When this technique flowers, your attention, your awareness, and your consciousness blossoms.

So, when you inhale, inhale deeply. When the breath turns, bring the awareness to that point. Do not try to hold the breath, if in that moment the breath by itself naturally takes time from inhale to exhale, that's fine, but don't force it. Let the attention be there. Similarly, when the breath moves from exhale to inhale, find yourself centered in that place, the fusion point.

This techniques helps you experience the stillness that can transcend your consciousness. Buddha only practiced this technique, this first technique from Vigyan Bhairav Tantra. He practiced this technique for years, and we know the awakening of Buddha, how he became a powerhouse of compassion and light to the world.

A river of light

Another beautiful technique from Vigyan Bhairav Tantra is visualizing a vast, bright light above your head. This vast, bright light is full of peace and serenity and purity. Imagine a vast, bright light filled with peace, beauty, serenity, a golden light or a peaceful bright moonlight. Visualise this light above your head entering through your head into your heart. Like a river flowing into your heart, flowing and expanding in your heart, enlightening, filling you with light, filling your heart with this bright light. A river of peace and serenity entering your heart space, the most inner core of your heart. Let this light reach to the deepest core of your heart. As you breathe, imagine this light flowing down through your body, eliminating every part, every part of your being, of your body, of your breath and settling in your heart, the vast light flowing from above your head to your heart and with the breath, deep breath it is going to every part, every aspect of your being and it will illuminating every core of your being, every part of your body and settling in your heart, settling in your being, a deep presence, vast universe, settling in your heart, enlightening, illuminating every aspect, every cell of your body, with this bright light, peaceful, full of vitality, full of life, full of blessings, illuminating every corner of your body, of your being and with the deep breath settling in your heart.

The gap between thoughts

Then Shiva says, O Shakti, bring your awareness, bring your attention to the gap between your thoughts. When one thought comes, from one thought to another thought, the gap, bring your attention to the gap, to that inner space in between two thoughts. Let your awareness, let your consciousness settle in that gap. Let thoughts pass, the attension stays with that brief pause between them, the space, though tiny, leads to a profound sense of silence, business and stillness, a deep sense of rest, silence and stillness.

A sense of balance, like a pristine lake, starts manifesting in one's self, with the practice of this technique. Trust that with time, the gap becomes bigger and bigger and bigger. In the beginning, even if there is a train of thoughts, one after another, or rumination of thoughts, one after another, find that gap.

Whether you find that gap when the breath turns, or you find the gap when one thought changes to another, pay attention to this gap, and with time this gap will grow into stillness, into deep peaceful silence, the isness of life itself.

Awareness of hara

Then Shiva says, oh Shakti, bring your awareness below the navel, just one to two inches below the navel, and there feel the centre of your being.

This is one of the finest and most practiced meditation techniques in the Zen monasteries, and it was the master technique for the samurais of Japan. The samurais were able to command great courage, great will through the power of this technique. They have a unique word for it, hara. Your hara, your centre below the navel. In the ancient Japan, they used to even consider this place where the heart is, where the life is. When samurais were asked, "where do you feel and think from?", they used to point to hara, just between one or two inches below the navel, two fingers below the navel. Hara, the centre of your being.

When you bring your attention to hara, the centre of your being, you are going to the very source of life in your body. This is also the place where we are connected to the mother, and it also happens to be the gravitational centre of our body. For animals walking on four feet, this centre is different. This gravitational centre changed for the humans when they started walking on two feet. When this centre changed, when the awareness of the human consciousness came to this centre, a transcendence happened, an evolution, a revolution happened in the being.

Shiva says, oh Shakti, bring your awareness to your hara, to your navel. Let your breath reach to your navel. When you breathe, breathe deep to and from through your navel. Let prana, let life energy, let chi reach to your navel. Let your attention and consciousness be centred in this place. When you're walking, pay attention to this centre near the navel or sit comfortably and bring your attention to the centre of your being at the heart of hara. Take deep breaths and feel a deep sense of centredness, awareness, power and presence emanating from your navel, from your hara. Let yourself be centred in this place. Once you centre here, you can rely on your will, on your presence.

Awareness in caress

Then Shiva says, oh Shakti, know the total awareness while being caressed and loved by your beloved. Enter that caress, that love is everlasting life. During any pleasant loving touch, immerse yourself into the sensation of that caress, of that love, embrace it and bring your attention to that embrace, to that loving caress, to that hug, to that touch. Immerse yourself in it and feel that everlasting sense of life and presence in that caress. Let the sense of touch, of care, of love become a guiding light to presence, to love, to beauty.

Awareness of thoughts

Then Shiva says, oh Shakti, be aware of your thoughts, watching your thoughts.

Watch the passing thoughts, pay attention to your thinking, to your thoughts. Don't touch it, don't change it, don't move it.

Just simple awareness, watchfulness, to your thoughts, pay attention, watch one thought comes, another goes, each thought with its own ideas, emotions, drama, emotions, feelings.

Just watch, pay attention, sit quietly and observe your thoughts without any attachment, without any pursuing these thoughts or running away from it, or habitually falling into the patterns of it, into the rumination of it.

Simply watch, one thought begins and it ends, maintaining this detached awareness throughout Ihipasyako, that's what Buddha called it, watch it as it is, without changing, without moving. Zazen, as they call it in Japan, just simply sitting, being, doing nothing.

Merging with the Earth

Here Shiva says, merge and melt with the Earth. Oh Shakti, lie down as dead in the grass, on the ground, and let the Earth hold you in its embrace. With open eyes, stare into the infinite without moving your eyelashes, but in the embrace of Earth. When hugging the earth, close your eyes and be one with the earth. This is a grounding technique, connecting you to the very heart of Mother Earth. Rest and settle in this, when you're lying on your belly, close your eyes and hug Mother Earth. Say thank you. Be in that restful state. When facing upwards, open your eyes and stare into the nothingness, playing dead, nothing exists.

One day we all reach to this place. Death has always kept its promise. It is there, it is sure. So, rest in this state for a moment, and let that restfulness, let that caress of the earth enter your being. Let this centering, grounding, and nurturing love of Mother Earth caress your body, caress your presence, caress your soul.

The vast universe

And Shiva says to Shakti, reflect on the vastness of this Universe. Imagine light rays coming from the base of your spine and rising upwards. Imagine an infinite powerhouse of energy at the base of your spine rising upwards. Rising upwards through every vertebra of your spine. Enlightening, illuminating all your centers through your heart and hands. Open your hands towards the sky, expand, and let this vast energy, this light reaching out to the vastness of this Universe.

When you practice this technique standing, have deep roots into the ground and let this vast reserve of energy, of light rise through your spine and expand through your heart and hands. Through your sahasthra, the center at the top of your head, through your eyes, reaching outwards to the vastness of this Universe.

See the vastness of this Universe, the infinite number

of stars, billions and billions of galaxies. Universe filled with life and beauty. Stars after stars, planets after planets, full of life, full of beauty, full of abundance. Vast magnificent Universe and you are part, you are one with this vastness. Melt and merge in this vastness. Let this vastness become part of you and you become part of it. Become one with this vastness.

This technique aligns all your energy centers and connects you directly to the vastness, to the richness and abundance of this Universe.

Embracing sound

Then Shiva says, oh Shakti, embrace the sound. The ancients call this mantra, and this has been a foundational technique for centuries, being transmitted from Guru to Shishya, from master to disciple.

Chant a sound loud. Pay awareness to the sound and embrace the sound into your heart and let the sound become more and more gentle. Let this chanting become inner without the outer sound from the throat. Pay attention to the inner chanting, observe it, watch it happening, let it happen by itself.

For more than 6,000 years, this has been one of the core

techniques. Every master has given this bhij mantra, this seed sound to his or her disciple. And a lineage has been created. It has been called the lineage of the mantra. In the 60s it became very popular, called Transcendental Meditation. The potent sound, your mantra, and you reflect on it.

Hari Om. More and more gentle. It becomes so soft, so subtle that your whole being becomes that sound. The sound becomes part of your heartbeat, becomes part of your breath, becomes part of your thoughts. It happens by itself. The sheer awareness, watchfulness of the sound, till the sound becomes the sound of the silence, a throbbing pulsating silence in your being.

Pranayama

Kapalabhati Pranayama

This is traditionally considered a cleansing exercise (shat kriya) rather than a pranayama. It is an easier version of the pranayama Bhastrika and is suitable for most levels of experience and fitness. Kapalbhati has many benefits. It cleanses the nasal passage, drains the sinuses, and eliminates accumulated mucus. It strengthens and increases the capacity of the lungs, removes bronchial congestion and spasms. It massages the abdominal organs through the movement of the diaphragm and abdominal contractions, strengthening the abdominal muscles and improving digestion. It refreshes and invigorates your mind and increases alertness due to increased flow of oxygen to your brain.

How to perform it:

- Find a comfortable sitting position, with your spine elongated.
- Take an abdominal breath in to prepare for pumping.
- Contract your abdominal muscles to exhale powerfully from the nose.

- Relax your abdominal muscles naturally, for inhalation.
- Be cautious not to inhale actively, but instead release your abdomen and allow the air to be sucked in passively.
- Repeat this for 3 sets. Increase pumping from 30 to 40 to 50 pumps per set.
- In between sets, take a deep breath, and release, then a gentle abdominal breath and retain the breath. Increase the duration from round to round. So first 20, then 30, and in the last round 40 seconds.

Bhastrika Pranayama

This Pranayama, also known as Bellows Breath, is a breathing exercise that mimics fanning a fire with a steady flow of air through actively filling and emptying the lungs and abdomen. This practice stokes the inner fire of the mind and body, supporting proper digestion on all levels, improving the lung function and reducing stress and anxiety.

How to do it:

- Choose a comfortable sitting position, resting the hands on the knees, and consciously opening the chest. Allow the spine to lengthen, close your eyes and breathe through the nose. Inhale fully, filling first the abdomen, then the lower thorax and lastly upper thorax with air, and then exhale powerfully, without strain or tension. As you exhale, allow the abdomen to dynamically contract, drawing the navel toward the spine as the diaphragm ascends toward the lungs.

- Follow this exhalation immediately with a powerful inhalation, without strain or tension. As you inhale, allow the abdomen to actively expand, moving the navel away from the spine as the diaphragm descends toward the pelvic floor.
- Continue this cycle of powerful inhalations and exhalations. Focus on both the inhale and the exhale; their length and force should remain equal as you practice.
- Observe the breath, the flow of prana, and your dynamic movements as you count ten of these dynamic breaths. At the top of the tenth inhalation, retain the breath for a moment before gently releasing the breath with a long, complete exhalation. Then, take one more deep inhalation and exhale slowly. This completes one round.

- If it feels natural, you can allow the hips and spine to gently rock forward with each inhalation, opening the front body, and then allow the hips to rock backwards as the spine contracts slightly on each exhalation. Keep the body relaxed throughout the exercise.
- When you begin doing Bhastrika, keep the breathing fairly slow, about one breath every two seconds. With practice, the abdominal muscles will grow stronger, and you can build up to five rounds—each consisting of ten forceful breaths, a brief pause at the top of the tenth inhalation, a long, slow exhale followed by one more deep inhalation and a slow exhalation.
- When you are ready to close your practice, complete a round with a long, relaxed breath in and out. Then allow your breath to return to normal.
- Notice how you feel. Notice your body. Notice your energy. Notice your thoughts and emotions.

Bhramari Pranayama

Bhramari Pranayama is a calming type pranayama with a soothing and healing effect on the mind. The technique is also known as Bumblebee Breath and Humming Bee Breath, named after the black bumblebee in India that has a deep buzz similar to the sound produced in Bhramari Breathing, where a humming sound is created while inhaling and exhaling through the nose. The sound is produced when your glottis, the space between your vocal cords, is actively constricted, and the humming creates a healing vibration that can help release tension and promote mental relaxation.

How to do it:

- In a comfortable seated position, close your ears with your index fingers.
- Place your index finger on the cartilage between your cheek and your ear. Your finger should not be inside your ear.
- Close your eyes and take a deep breath in through your nostrils. As you breathe in, slightly contract your glottis and gently engage your vocal cords to create a light snoring sound.
- Breathe in slowly and comfortably, and at the same time, create this snoring sound.
- Once you have completed your inhalation, breathe out slowly while creating a humming sound.

- Create this hum in your nose and visualize piercing your third eye chakra in between your eyebrows with it.
- Repeat six to eight times and close with an extended exhalation.

Anulom Vilom Pranayama

This a one of the core breathing exercises. It involves conscious breath regulation by inhaling through one nostril while keeping the other closed.

With practice of Anulom Vilom, the nervous system is cleansed, and the practice also improves blood circulation which makes it ideal for the heart.

How to do it:

- Sit comfortably. Keep the waist, back, neck and spine erect.
- Inhaling and exhaling should be slow and noiseless. You can gradually increase the time for inhalation and exhalation, but keep the breathing exercise easy and enjoy it. Do not stress your breathing too much.
- For closing the right nostril, press with right hand thumb. For closing the left right nostril, press with

the ring finger of the right hand. Keep the other hand on your knee.

- Inhale slowly through the left nostril and fill your lungs to maximum capacity. Exhale slowly through the right nostril, inhale again through the right nostril, and exhale again through the left nostril. This is one set.
- Repeat five sets. You can gradually increase to ten-twenty sets.
- Pay attention to the rhythm of the breathing and feel the flow of prana throughout your body.
- When you have practiced for 2-3 months, you can practice retention of breath. Keep the ratio of inhalation, retention of breath and exhalation 1:4:2. For starters, do not hold the breath, and keep the ratio of inhalation-exhalation to (1:2).

Osho Active Meditations

"Just sitting directly in silence won't help. The moment you sit silently, you will see all sorts of things moving inside you; you will feel it almost impossible to be silent. First throw those things out so you come to a natural state of rest. Real meditation starts only when you are at rest."

—OSHO - The Discipline of Transcendence, Vol. 2, Discourse 5

Osho Active Meditations are transformative experiences designed to help you break free from stress and emotional blockages, allowing you to dive deep into a state of serene awareness and joy. By incorporating physical movements and expressive actions, they bring you to a place of profound stillness and clarity.

Here's a guide to some of Osho's most powerful active meditations. The music for the Active Meditations is available online and on different streaming services.

Dynamic Meditation

Imagine starting your day by unleashing all your pent-up energy and emotions, shaking off any lingering sleepiness, and bursting into your full potential. Dynamic Meditation is a journey of five stages that lasts for 60 minutes and leaves you feeling vibrant and alive:

— **Breathing** (10 minutes): Begin with chaotic, fast breathing through your nose, energizing your body and clearing your mind.

— **Expressing** (10 minutes): Scream, laugh, cry, jump, or whatever comes naturally to you in this moment—let go of everything holding you back.

— **Chanting** (10 minutes): With arms raised, jump and shout "Hoo!" – feel the powerful vibrations fill you with vitality.

— **Witnessing** (15 minutes): Stand or sit in stillness, observing the inner silence that follows the storm.

— **Celebrating** (15 minutes): Dance joyously, embracing the new-found freedom and lightness in your being.

Kundalini Meditation

Shed your stress like a snake sheds its skin, emerging renewed and peaceful. Kundalini Meditation, practiced in the late afternoon, is a 60-minute journey to deep relaxation and inner peace:

— **Shaking** (15 minutes): Let your body shake naturally, releasing tension and freeing your energy.

— **Dancing** (15 minutes): Dance however you feel, expressing your emotions and energies without inhibition.

— **Witnessing** (15 minutes): Sit or stand in silence, feeling the serene calmness within.

— **Relaxing** (15 minutes): Lie down, completely relaxed, allowing the tranquility to wash over you.

Nataraj Meditation

Loose yourself in the dance, feeling every cell in your body vibrate with joy and freedom. Nataraj Meditation is a 65-minute journey that transforms movement into meditation:

— **Dancing** (40 minutes): Dance as if nobody is watching, immerse yourself in the rhythm, and let your body move as it wishes.

— **Witnessing** (20 minutes): Lie down in silence, absorbing the stillness that follows the dance.

— **Celebrating** (5 minutes): Dance once more, this time with celebration, feeling the ecstasy of pure, unfiltered joy.

Nadabrahma Meditation

Imagine resonating with the sound of the universe, your entire being humming with peace and balance. Nadabrahma Meditation is a 60-minute practice that uses sound and hand movements to bring you into harmony:

— **Humming** (30 minutes): Sit comfortably, close your eyes, and hum, letting the vibrations fill your body and soul.

— **Hand Movements** (15 minutes): Move your hands in slow circles, first outward then inward, balancing your energy.

— **Witnessing** (15 minutes): Sit in silence, feeling the deep sense of harmony and oneness with the universe.

These meditations are not just practices but powerful journeys that can elevate your everyday life. Embrace them with an open heart and experience the profound transformation they can bring.

Bījamantra

Bījamantras, or seed mantras, are powerful, monosyllabic sounds that are supportive in invoking different energies from the world of archetypes. These sacred syllables are used for the invocation of deities or to activate the chakras within the body. Each Bījamantra encapsulates the essence of the deity it invokes, channeling their divine energy and blessings.

For instance, the Bījamantra for Ma Shakti is "Hreem," which harmonizes the energies of both Shiva and Shakti, embodying their divine union. "Shreem," the Bījamantra for Ma Lakshmi, resonates with the vibrations of abundance and prosperity, inviting her blessings into one's life. The Bījamantra "Ayeim" for Ma Saraswati channels the flow of knowledge and creativity, guiding one towards enlightenment. "Doom," the Bījamantra for Ma Durga, embodies her strength and ability to bring order to chaos. Lastly, "Kleem" and "Kreem," the Bījamantras for Ma Kali, are gateways to her transformative power, cutting through ignorance and leading to profound spiritual awakening.

These seed sounds can be chanted on their own or as part of more elaborate mantras, enhancing their spiritual potency. As one immerses in the vibration of these Bījamantras, they align with the divine forces they represent, invoking their blessings and transforming both inner and outer life.

For the best effect, one should be initiated into these mantras.